AM I TOO YOUNG?

Lessons from young Bible characters with reflections and faith declarations

IJEOMA OKOLIE

©2021—Ijeoma Okolie

All rights reserved.

This book is protected by the copyright laws of the United Kingdom. No part of this publication may be reproduced, distributed, or transmitted in any form or by any means, or stored in a database or retrieval system, without the prior written permission of the author.

ISBN: 978-1-5262-0886-6

Unless otherwise indicated, all Scripture is taken from the Holy Bible: Easy-to-Read Version (ERV), International Edition ©2012, 2016 by Bible League International and used by permission.

Also used: King James Version which is public domain.

Published by:
Red Stripes Ltd.

Printed by:

Book Cover Design, Editing and Interior Design by:
Omotayo Koleosho
omotayokoleoshothewritingcoach@gmail.com

Printed in the United Kingdom

Dedication

To GOD my Heavenly Father, thank you for your overwhelming love and for giving me the wonderful opportunity to start this project.
I am so grateful, dear Lord!

Psalm 9:1
I will praise you, Lord, with all my heart.
I will tell about the wonderful things you have done.

Acknowledgements

To my parents Sir Anele & Lady Azuka Uwanaka. Thank you for all your love and support, for raising my siblings and I in the way of the Lord and for giving us a solid foundation in Christ. I appreciate your continuous prayers and encouragement.

To my dear husband Emeka, I am grateful for your commitment through the years. I appreciate you.

To my bright and delightful children, Chisomebi and Enyinna, for the joy you bring into my life, I am grateful. Being your mum has given me a whole different perspective to life.

To my siblings, Chukweks, Uchechi, Chinenye and Ebube. Thank you for all the different ways you have been a blessing to me.

To Esther, for your encouragement and for holding me accountable I am grateful. Thank you for all you do raising God's daughters and in nation building.

To Adeola, 'big sis', for just being there for me, I am grateful. Thank you for all your support and encouragement through my journey, for all you do in the kingdom, and for building and equipping members of the body Christ globally.

To Mrs A, for the impact you have had in my life, I appreciate you. Thank you for raising armies and transformational leaders for God's kingdom all over the world.

Contents

INTRODUCTION	i
JACOB AND ESAU	1
JOSEPH	13
MIRIAM, THE SISTER OF MOSES	32
SAMUEL	40
DAVID	50
KING JEHOASH/JOASH	67
KING AZARIAH/UZZIAH	80
KING MANASSEH	89
KING JOSIAH	97
ELISHA AND THE YOUTH	108

NAAMAN'S SERVANT GIRL	118
ESTHER	124
JEREMIAH	142
DANIEL	150
THE BOY WITH BREAD AND FISHES	175
RHODA THE SERVANT GIRL	183
TIMOTHY	190
MARY, THE MOTHER OF JESUS	199
JESUS	211
CONCLUSION	241

Introduction

I have had a relationship with Jesus since I was young and it has been and still is a wonderful and fulfilling experience. Having Christ in me and allowing the Holy Spirit to lead me, is my hope of living in the fullness of God.

My journey as a Christian wasn't always perfect growing up, but even when I made mistakes, I didn't stay down because God helped me rise above them.

Building on my foundation of faith and knowledge in Christ from my childhood has helped me navigate challenging circumstances. He still keeps me going — it's not a one off; it's a lifestyle.

I have been intentional about growing a healthy relationship with the Lord by making the right choices. From choosing — the books I read, the programs I watch on TV, the music I listen to, the friends and company I keep and more — all have helped me grow in Christ.
I am grateful for God's grace that has helped me remain steadfast.

I have learned that no matter the challenges you face in life, no matter how messy the situation is, yield yourself to God. Take the mistakes to him and he will use it for his glory.

Surrender the pain, hurts, disappointments, and discouragements to God. He will heal and restore you. He wants a willing vessel. I have completely and wholeheartedly surrendered to him. Will you do the same?

So when you agree to the process, God makes His grace available for you. He helps and provides the support and people you need in the journey of your life. He also removes things and people he knows would hinder you from being who he has called and made you to be. But you have to make that choice!

As a Sunday school teacher, I derive a lot of joy from teaching young ones the scripture. The ways their eyes light up when they discover who they are in Christ and the possibilities they can become brings such joy to my heart.
Now I understand why the scripture tells us to receive the word of God with childlike faith. That faith is so pure.

Luke 18: 17 The truth is, you must accept God's kingdom like a little child accepts things, or you will never enter it."

Why write this book?

Because you are very important and relevant and I believe the Lord wants the youth to cultivate a personal relationship with him, so they can know God themselves.

Dear reader, never believe the lie that there is a perfect life because it simply does not exist. Jesus tells us in the scriptures that we would have trials in this world, but we should take heart and rejoice because he has overcome them all. As you go through your beautiful life, do not be discouraged and do not give up when you are faced with a challenge, because Jesus will see you through just as he has promised.

This book is an opportunity for you to know that regardless of where you are, be it in a palace or in austere situations, there is hope for you to thrive and be all God has made and called you to be.

We make choices and decisions every day of our lives. Some of these choices will change our lives forever while others will be more or less insignificant to who we become. You and I are a product of our daily choices!

I have read about some of 'God's Generals' who encountered Christ as teenagers. Presently, I know and have personal relationships with great women and men in the faith that had encounters with God as young people. So I know that you should not despise your journey of faith even as a youth. What you do now may seem like little steps but they are in the right direction.

I hope you will not see yourself as worthless — you will not look down on who God has made you to be.

Zechariah 4:10a Do not despise these small beginnings, for the Lord rejoices to see the work begin.

Although the chapters of the book are a combination of the experiences of male and female characters, it is not restrictive, because you can learn from both.

Each chapter of this book involves a story of a bible character, some highlights and lessons. The lessons I have shared are not exhaustive — you are free to add yours in the notes at the end of each chapter or in your personal journal.
There are too many mysteries in God that cannot be summarised in a book, so allow God to teach you more as he opens you up to insights in him. It is an unfolding map, so please come back and read again and again.

We should meditate on God's word day and night so we can be transformed. You have the opportunity to either ponder and personally reflect on your learnings, or share your thoughts with others.

At the end of each chapter, make the declarations over yourself.
You may wonder, why make faith confessions?

When you speak God's word continually into your life, you will see yourself transform into all that God has purposed for you. Because you are speaking life over yourself.

Proverbs 18:21 The tongue can speak words that bring life or death. Those who love to talk must be ready to accept what it brings.

There are also bible scriptures included for your further readings. You can choose any version of the bible to read and learn more.

This book can be used during your personal study or during a group study with other believers. I encourage you to engage in conversations from the book with your family, friends, and faith leaders. Ask them questions on areas you are unsure about.

As you read this book, may you taste and see that God is indeed good. I pray that you have a personal revelation of God and he will be so real to you, that you would not have to depend on another person's experience of God

Each day of your life, you will make all around progress and be all God has called you to be.
I pray you see yourself and others through God's perspective.

May the eyes of your heart be enlightened, so that you will know and cherish the hope to which God has called you. I hope you see all the possibilities you can be in Christ, and all the great things God can do in and through you.

In Jesus name, Amen.

Jeremiah 1

4 The Lord's message came to me:
5 "Before I made you in your mother's womb,
I knew you.
Before you were born,
    I chose you for a special work.
    I chose you to be a prophet to the nations."
6 Then I said, "But, Lord God, I do not know how to speak. I am only a boy."
7 But the Lord said to me,
"Don't say, 'I am only a boy.'
    You must go everywhere I send you
    and say everything I tell you to say.
8 Don't be afraid of anyone.
    I am with you, and I will protect you."
This message is from the Lord.

1 Timothy 4:12

Don't let anyone look down on you because you are young, but set an example for the believers in speech, in conduct, in love, in faith and in purity.
This was Paul's instruction to Timothy.

JACOB AND ESAU

Abraham and Sarah had a son called Issac. Issac married Rebekah as his wife. Rebekah could not have children, so Issac prayed to the Lord for her to conceive and the Lord heard Isaac's prayer. Rebekah got pregnant!
While Rebekah was pregnant, the babies inside her belly struggled with one another.

She prayed to the Lord and asked, "What is happening to me?"

The Lord said to her, "The leaders of two nations are in your body. Two nations will come from you, and they will be divided. One of them will be stronger, and the older will serve the younger."

When it was time for Rebekah to deliver, she had twin boys. The first baby boy was red and his skin was like a hairy robe. So he was named Esau. When the second baby was born, he was holding on to Esau's heel tightly.

So that baby was named Jacob. Isaac, their father, was sixty years old when the twin boys, Jacob and Esau were born.

The boys grew up. Esau became a skilled hunter, who loved to be out in the fields. But Jacob was a quiet man, who stayed at home. Isaac loved Esau, so he enjoyed eating the animals Esau killed. But Rebekah loved Jacob. These twin brothers had very different characters and personalities. One was outgoing, while the other was not. There is nothing wrong with this because you need to stay true to who God made you to be.

Imagine how risky and adventurous being a hunter like Esau was. He was always out in the fields and forest chasing animals, to kill for food. He mastered hunting, and with constant practice, he became skillful at it.
Jacob on the other hand was quite possibly a thinker that was at home studying and learning. However, he was quite courageous as we would see in subsequent actions.

One day, Esau came back from hunting, tired and weak from hunger. He met Jacob cooking a pot of stew. Esau said to Jacob, "I am weak with hunger. Let me have some of that red stew." (That is why people call him "Edom", the Hebrew word for "Red.").

Jacob replied his twin brother, "You must sell me your rights as the firstborn son."

Esau said, "I am almost dead with hunger, so what good are these rights to me now?"

Jacob replied, "First, promise me that you will give them to me."

Esau made an oath to him and sold his rights as the firstborn son to Jacob. Jacob then gave Esau some bread and lentil stew. Esau ate the food, had something to drink, and then left. With his actions, Esau showed that he did not care about his rights as the firstborn son.
The twin brothers grew older, and so did their father, Issac. Issac was so old that his eyes became weak and he could not see clearly.

He called Esau and said to him, "Prepare my favourite meal and bring it to me and I will eat it. Then I will bless you before I die."

Esau obeyed his father and went hunting. While he was out hunting, Jacob, with the help of his mother, tricked his father Issac and received Esau's blessings.

Esau was very upset with Jacob. What he did not understand was he had already sold his birthright to his brother, Jacob, for food. He did not realise that there was a price to pay for being indifferent to his birthright. He let go of his special honour for temporary pleasure. Esau hated Jacob because he tricked him and took his blessing.

Jacob had to run from his twin brother Esau, because he feared he would kill him. Many years after Jacob fled from Esau, God blessed him. Jacob had two wives, two maidservants, one daughter and twelve sons. Esau on the other hand, had four wives and five children, because God also blessed him.

One day, God asked Jacob to return to his country. He was afraid to go back because he thought his brother Esau would still be angry with him and attack him even after so many years. Jacob prayed to God to save him from his brother and God answered his prayers. He got special gifts for his brother to show him how sorry he was. Jacob sent these gifts with his servants ahead of him to his twin brother, Esau. He gave the servants instructions on what to say and do when they met Esau. That night, Jacob sent his family and everything he owned across the river.

Genesis 32

24 Jacob was left alone, and a man came and wrestled with him. The man fought with him until the sun came up. 25 When the man saw that he could not defeat Jacob, he touched Jacob's leg and put it out of joint.
26 Then the man said to Jacob, "Let me go. The sun is coming up."
But Jacob said, "I will not let you go. You must bless me."

27 And the man said to him, "What is your name?" And Jacob said, "My name is Jacob."
28 Then the man said, "Your name will not be Jacob. Your name will now be Israel. I give you this name because you have fought with God and with men, and you have won."
29 Then Jacob asked him, "Please tell me your name." But the man said, "Why do you ask my name?" Then the man blessed Jacob at that place.
30 So Jacob named that place Peniel. He said, "At this place, I saw God face to face, but my life was spared."
31 Then the sun came up as Jacob left Peniel. He was limping because of his leg.
32 So even today, the people of Israel do not eat the muscle that is on the hip joint, because this is the muscle where Jacob was hurt.

When Esau saw his twin brother, he ran and threw his arms around Jacob and kissed him. They hugged each other, cried and reconciled.

Esau had moved his whole clan — wives, sons, daughters, all his livestock including goods — from Canaan to the hill country of Seir, a country far away from his brother Jacob. Esau and Jacob could not live in the same country because their possessions were so much.

Esau had five sons named Eliphaz, Reuel, Jeush, Jaalam and Korah. Esau and his entire family lived in Mount Seir, and he became the father of the Edomites. God appeared to Jacob again;

Genesis 35

10 and said to him, "Your name is Jacob, but I will change that name. You will no longer be called Jacob. Your new name will be Israel." So God named him Israel.

11 God said to him, "I am God All-Powerful, and I give you this blessing: Have many children and grow into a great nation. Other nations and other kings will come out of you.

12 I gave Abraham and Isaac some special land. Now I give the land to you and to all your people who will live after you."

13 Then God left that place.

14-15 Jacob set up a memorial stone there. He made the rock holy by pouring wine and oil on it. This was a special place because God spoke to Jacob there, and Jacob named the place Bethel.

Jacob, whose name had now become Israel, lived in the land of Canaan with his family. He had twelve sons named Reuben, Simeon, Levi, Judah, Issachar, Zebulun,

Dan, Naphtali, Joseph, Benjamin, Gad, Asher and a daughter named Dinah. During the season of famine God told Israel to move to Egypt with his entire family and all their possessions. At the time, his son, Joseph, was already a Governor in Egypt. God gave them favour before the Egyptian king, Pharaoh and the descendants of Israel, known as the Israelites, settled in Goshen, a region in the country of Egypt.

Israel lived seventeen years in Egypt and he died at a hundred and forty seven years after blessing his sons and giving them instructions.

Further reading: Genesis 25 & 27 , 32, 33, 35-37.

☀ Highlights

IMPATIENCE - If Esau was a bit more patient, he would not have sold his birthright, and would have still had a meal. Do not trivialise important decisions and choices in your life, so you do not have regrets in the future. Patience is a desirable virtue and you can ask God to help you become patient, or more patient where needed. Even when you find yourself in a desperate situation, it is important to make wise choices.

PERSONALITY - Everyone has their unique, God-given personality. You can't change it, but you can master it and improve upon it. Someone who is naturally quiet should accept who they are, and someone who is naturally outspoken should also accept themselves.

Your environment involves not just family and school, but also the friends you make, the books you read, the music you listen to as well as the programs you watch. Hence, it is important to be in a positive and healthy environment to have a positive attitude.

SIBLING RIVALRY - I personally wonder how long Jacob had been desiring Esau's birthright. Or did he think about it the moment Esau asked him for some stew? He was quiet yet so ambitious! A healthy relationship with our siblings is important, even from childhood. As you grow older together, your sibling bond gets stronger.

REPENTANCE AND FORGIVENESS - After many years, Jacob's life experiences changed him to a better man. He realised he had to reconcile with his brother Esau, and he did. As you get older, it is expected that you become wiser, because you learn from your past victories and mistakes and make amends where needed. Jacob prayed and asked the Lord to save him from any of his brother's attacks and God helped him. When Esau saw Jacob after many years he forgave him and he reconciled with his brother. Ask God to help you if you struggle with forgiving yourself or others.

Ponder

- What is my personality?

- Am I learning more about myself? What are my likes and dislikes?

- In what ways can I improve myself to be the best version of me?

- Do I reconcile with others when they offend me?

- Is there someone I need to forgive?

🗣 Declare

- I make wise decisions at all times.

- I have a healthy relationship with others.

- I forgive quickly and freely.

- I am grateful for who God made me.

- I will be the best version of myself.

MY NOTES

MY NOTES

JOSEPH

Joseph was a favoured son and more loved than his brothers. He was born at a time when his father Jacob, whose name was changed to Israel by an angel of the Lord, was very old. His mother's name was Rachel and he was the eleventh son of Israel. The names of his older brothers were; Reuben, Simeon, Levi, Judah, Dan, Naphtali, Gad, Asher, Issachar, Zebulun and he had a younger brother called Benjamin.

Israel made Joseph a tunic — a special coat — of many colours. This showed how special and precious Joseph was to his father, Israel. Joseph respected his father, so whenever his brothers did any bad thing, he told his father. His brothers knew their father loved him very much. It made them jealous of him and they hated him.

Joseph as a seventeen year old teenager was responsible for taking care of his father's goats and sheep. One day, while he was out of the house, working in the field and feeding the flock with his brothers, Joseph shared a special dream that he had with his brothers.

Joseph said, "I had a dream last night. We were all working in the field, tying stacks of wheat together. Then my stack got up. It stood there while all of your stacks of wheat made a circle around mine and bowed down to it."

Joseph was young and did not understand his dream at that time but his brothers who were older understood it.

So they asked him "Do you think this means that you will be a king and rule over us?"

Joseph's dream made his brothers hate him even more. Joseph had another dream, and he told his brothers about it.

He said, "I had another dream. I saw the sun, the moon, and eleven stars bowing down to me."

Joseph also told his father about this dream, but his father criticised him, "What kind of dream is this? Do you believe that your mother, your brothers, and I will bow down to you?" Joseph's brothers continued to be jealous of him, but his father thought about all these things and wondered what they could mean.

Joseph was a very confident boy, but he did not understand the meaning of his dreams, nor did he understand that they made his brothers annoyed.
Although Joseph did not understand what his dreams meant, the details of his dreams gave a glimpse into the future God had planned for him.

When we pray and ask God, he gives us the interpretation and understanding of our night dreams and visions.

One day, when Joseph's brothers went out to take care of their father's sheep, his father sent him to go see if his brothers were safe at Shechem, but on the way Joseph got lost. A man found him wandering in the fields.

The man asked, "What are you looking for?"

Joseph answered, "I am looking for my brothers. Can you tell me where they are with their sheep?"

The man asked, "They have already gone away. I heard them say that they were going to Dothan."

So Joseph followed his brothers and found them in Dothan. His brothers saw him coming towards them from a far distance and they said to one another, "Here comes Joseph the dreamer."

They were so jealous of him and his dreams that they

planned how they would kill their own brother. Rueben however insisted that his brothers do not kill Joseph. When Joseph came close to his brothers, they attacked him and tore his special coat of many colours. They put him in a dry empty well while they ate. Not long after, they looked ahead and saw a group of Ishmaelite traders on their camels from Gilead heading to Egypt. Judah then advised his other brothers that they gained nothing if they killed their own brother Joseph. Instead, it was better if they sold him as a slave to the Ishmaelite traders. It was true that they hated their brother, however they did not want to live with the guilt of killing him.

Imagine how Joseph must have felt being attacked by his own brothers whom he loved even though he did nothing wrong to them. He must have felt so betrayed.

Joseph was sold into slavery in Egypt for twenty shekels of silver. His brothers deceived their father and told him a wild animal had killed Joseph because they dipped his torn coat in the blood of a goat they had slaughtered. Israel was hurt. He mourned Joseph and he could not be comforted.

He was sold as a slave in Egypt to Potiphar, an officer of Pharaoh and Captain of the guards. Egypt was very different from the land of Canaan where he lived. It was more modern, civilised, and they spoke a different language too.

Slavery has long been abolished but back in those days, human beings could be slaves and they were regarded as legal property of their owner who bought them to work for their owners. They had no rights to be free persons. Joseph lived with his rich master, Potiphar and his wife. Potiphar liked Joseph. He saw that God was with Joseph and made him successful, so he made Joseph a ruler over everything. From the time Joseph became the ruler in charge of Potiphar's house, God blessed everything in his master's house and everything that grew in his field. Potiphar did not have to worry about anything except deciding what he ate.

Joseph was a handsome and good looking young man. After some time, the wife of Joseph's master began to pay special attention to him, and tried to tempt him. One day she said to him, "Sleep with me."

Joseph refused, "My master trusts me with everything in his house. He has given me responsibility for everything here except you, his wife. I cannot sleep with his wife. That is wrong! It is a sin against God."

Potiphar's wife would not take no for an answer. She kept bothering him every day, but he refused to sleep with her.

One day, Joseph went into the house to do his work. He was the only man in the house at the time. His master's wife came to him, grabbed his coat and said, "Come to bed with me."

Joseph was shocked and ran out of the house so fast that he left his coat in her hands.

She felt disappointed and called out to the men outside, "Look! This Hebrew slave was brought here to make fun of us. He came in and tried to attack me, but I screamed." She continued to lie, "My scream scared him and he ran away, but he left his coat with me."

She kept his coat until her husband, Potiphar, came home. She told her husband the same story. She said, "This Hebrew slave you brought here tried to attack me! But when he came near me, I screamed. He ran away, but he left his coat."

Potiphar was so angry that he put Joseph in prison, a place where the king's prisoners were held.

Joseph must have been in deep thought about how unfair it was that so many bad things had happened to him in his young life. He must have wondered what the future held for him.
However, even while he was in prison, God was with Joseph and continued to show kindness to him. The commander of the prison guards began to like Joseph. He put Joseph in charge of all the prisoners. Although Joseph was the leader of prisoners, he still did the same work they all did.

As a young prisoner, he had good character regardless of where he was. The commander of the guards trusted Joseph because the Lord was with Joseph and made him successful in everything he did.

Some time passed, and while Joseph was still in prison, Pharaoh the King of Egypt threw his butler — wine server — and baker into prison because they offended him. The commander put the two prisoners under Joseph's care. One night, the baker and butler each had a dream that had its own meaning. The next morning, Joseph noticed they were worried and asked, "Why do you look so worried today?"

The two men answered, "We both had dreams last night, but we do not understand what they mean. There is no one to explain the dreams to us."

Joseph said to them, "God is the only one who can understand and explain dreams. So I beg you, tell me your dreams."

With God's help, Joseph was able to interpret dreams. He had grown and developed his faith in God. This helped him interpret dreams accurately. He explained to the Butler and the baker what their dreams meant and it happened to them just as Joseph explained.

Joseph told the butler to remember him when he is free, and to also be good and be of help to him, "Tell Pharaoh me so that I can get out of this prison because I was kidnapped and taken from the land of the Hebrews. I have done nothing wrong and I should not be in prison."

When the butler got out of prison, he forgot about Joseph and said nothing about him to Pharaoh the King. Two years later, something huge happened. Pharaoh, the king of Egypt had two dreams that troubled him. The king shared his dreams with his wise men and magicians in the palace but none of them could interpret the dreams. It was then the King's butler remembered Joseph in the prison and how he could explain the king's dream to him. Pharaoh called for Joseph and the guards quickly got Joseph out of prison. Joseph shaved, put on some clean clothes, and went to see Pharaoh.

Pharaoh said to Joseph, "I had a dream, and no one can explain it for me. I heard that you can explain dreams when someone tells you about them."

Joseph answered, "I cannot, but God can explain the dream for you, Pharaoh."

Genesis 41 (KJV)
15 And Pharaoh said unto Joseph, I have dreamed a dream, and there is none that can interpret it: and I have heard say of thee, that when thou hearest a dream thou canst interpret it.

16 And Joseph answered Pharaoh, saying, It is not in me: God shall give Pharaoh an answer of peace.

17 And Pharaoh spake unto Joseph, In my dream, behold, I stood upon the brink of the river:

18 and, behold, there came up out of the river seven kine, fatfleshed and well favoured; and they fed in the reed-grass:

19 and, behold, seven other kine came up after them, poor and very ill favoured and leanfleshed, such as I never saw in all the land of Egypt for badness:

20 and the lean and ill favoured kine did eat up the first seven fat kine:

21 and when they had eaten them up, it could not be known that they had eaten them; but they were still ill favoured, as at the beginning. So I awoke.

22 And I saw in my dream, and, behold, seven ears came up upon one stalk, full and good:

23 and, behold, seven ears, withered, thin, and blasted with the east wind, sprung up after them:

24 and the thin ears swallowed up the seven good ears: and I told it unto the magicians; but there was none that could declare it to me.

25 And Joseph said unto Pharaoh, The dream of

Pharaoh is one: what God is about to do he hath declared unto Pharaoh.

26 The seven good kine are seven years; and the seven good ears are seven years: the dream is one.

27 And the seven lean and ill favoured kine that came up after them are seven years, and also the seven empty ears blasted with the east wind; they shall be seven years of famine.

28 That is the thing which I spake unto Pharaoh: what God is about to do he hath shewed unto Pharaoh.

29 Behold, there come seven years of great plenty throughout all the land of Egypt:

30 and there shall arise after them seven years of famine; and all the plenty shall be forgotten in the land of Egypt; and the famine shall consume the land;

31 and the plenty shall not be known in the land by reason of that famine which followeth; for it shall be very grievous.

32 And for that the dream was doubled unto Pharaoh twice, it is because the thing is established by God, and God will shortly bring it to pass.

33 Now therefore let Pharaoh look out a man discreet and wise, and set him over the land of Egypt.

34 Let Pharaoh do this, and let him appoint overseers over the land, and take up the fifth part of the land of Egypt in the seven plenteous years.

35 And let them gather all the food of these good years that come, and lay up corn under the hand of Pharaoh for food in the cities, and let them keep it.

36 And the food shall be for a store to the land against the seven years of famine, which shall be in the land of Egypt; that the land perish not through the famine.

Joseph explained the meaning of the king's dreams to him and advised the king on what to do. The advice was a good idea to Pharaoh and all his officials. Then Pharaoh told them, "I do not think we can find anyone better than Joseph to take this job. God's Spirit is in him, making him very wise!"

Joseph was only thirty years old when Pharaoh made Joseph a Governor over all the land of Egypt and gave him the name Zaphenath-Paneah. Pharaoh gave his special ring which had his royal seal to Joseph. He also gave Joseph a fine linen robe, put a gold chain around his neck and gave him a chariot to ride on. Joseph got married to a woman called Asenath and they gave birth to two sons whom they named Manasseh and Ephraim.

A few years later, just as Joseph had said, there was a

famine in many lands including Egypt and Canaan, where Joseph's family lived. During the famine, Joseph's ten brothers came to buy some food in Egypt, because Egypt was the only land that had enough food stored, thanks to Joseph's godly wisdom. They bowed down to greet Joseph with their faces to the ground. Joseph recognised them but they did not recognise him. At first, he acted like he did not know them. However, after some time, he eventually revealed his identity and forgave his brothers. He looked after them and their families. He also took care of his father Jacob and comforted him in old age till his father died.

God promoted Joseph and made him a great man. God sent Joseph to Egypt to preserve the tribe of Israel during severe famine. Joseph was a lord in Egypt. God made him a father to Pharaoh and a lord of his whole household. He was also the ruler of Egypt. Joseph lived for a hundred and ten years before he went to be with the Lord.

Further reading; Genesis 37,39-50.

☀ Highlights

DREAMS - There is no one that is too young to hear and connect with God. One of the ways God still speaks to us is through dreams and visions, just like he did back then. God gives us the meaning of our dreams when we pray and ask him. Remember to share those dreams with a trusted adult that believes in God. You can share with them the key actions and your key emotions in the dream. You should consider the situation you were in or what you were thinking about before you slept. These will help your parent(s) or guardian(s) analyse your dream.

You should also be careful about the entertainment you watch and what you read. Ensure it is not something that makes you fearful or gives you negative emotions because these can affect what you dream about. Before bedtime at night, talk to your parent(s) or guardian(s) about anything that is disturbing you.

When you've had a bad dream or a nightmare, remember you have authority in the name of Jesus to rebuke anyone or situation that has troubled or is troubling you.

JEALOUSY - This is an unhealthy emotion to have. When you feel jealous, you need to deal with the jealousy immediately. Understanding and accepting your siblings and friends for who God has made them to

be is important for you to get along with them.
Be mindful and aware of the information you share with others and how you share such information.

CHALLENGES - Even if you have the best character, you will still face some challenges. Remain faithful because God sees you even when others do not see you and he rewards us all. Joseph had a good character that was clearly seen while he was in slavery in his master's house, in the prison, and even when he became Governor.

Regardless of the situation or challenges Joseph faced, God was with Joseph and kept him safe.
No matter your present challenges or difficulties, God is with you. He holds the future so do not give up!

DILIGENCE - God blesses and rewards good work and hard-work with promotion and success, so do not be lazy!

Joseph's gift, which was interpreting dreams, brought him to the king. He trained and developed the gift God gave him so it became useful to serve others. He didn't just interpret the king's dreams, he also gave the king a strategy that worked. A person's gift opens doors for him or her and brings them before great and important people. When you discover your gift, continue to develop and master it, so that you can be ready — when the opportunity comes — to use it to serve for God's glory.

INTEGRITY - Joseph had to run from committing sin against God, no matter what it cost him. He did not bother going back for his coat.

When you find situations that would tempt you to sin against God, just flee. Don't try to negotiate your way out of it. God hates sin so as his children we should hate sin too and run away from it by all means.

If Joseph thought he could pull a fast one on his master, and lay with his wife, he may not have become a Governor. Overcoming trials and temptations is all part of spiritual growth. Just as God was with Joseph through his challenges, he is with you too. Trust him to see you through any temptations you are facing or may face because he will see you through.

FORGIVENESS - Joseph forgave his brothers. He had many reasons to hate and treat them badly. As a Governor in Egypt, he could have had his revenge on his brothers for selling him into slavery but he did not. Instead, he forgave them and showed them love.

You should love others and forgive freely. Even when they do not apologise, choose to forgive them regardless.

FAITH - Joseph had great faith in God even when he did not have his parents with him. He trusted God to see him through.

The more you read and learn about God, the more you allow your faith in Him to grow.

SUCCESS - As long as God was with Joseph, he prospered.

Hence, true success comes from God. God blessed and favoured Joseph in his master's house as a slave. As a prisoner in jail, God was with him. When it was time for his rulership, God used Pharaoh to make him Governor in Egypt. You are blessed when you trust God and have confidence in him. So why not share your plans and activities with God, so he can bless them.

Ponder

- Am I too young to ask God the meaning of my dreams? The interpretation of dreams comes from God.

- When I have dreams, do I have a trusted guardian I can speak to about it?

- Do I feel jealous of someone or others and what makes me jealous?

- Am I aware of what I say to others and how it makes them feel?

- Am I aware that trying to cover up a lie so I do not get into trouble is deceitful?

- How do I relate with my siblings? Am I patient with them?

- Do I know what my talents and gifts are and how can I develop them?

Declare

- I am confident in who God has made me to be and I admire others without being jealous.

- Lord you are with me and I am a success.

- I find favour with God and other people.

- People are blessed because of me.

- God helps me stay honest even when I am tempted.

- I have good character no matter the challenges I face in life. I will trust God because I know he will see me through it.

- I have a healthy relationship with my sibling(s).

- I develop my gifts and talents and I use them to serve others.

MY NOTES

MY NOTES

MIRIAM, THE SISTER OF MOSES

Miriam was the sister of Moses and Aaron. Moses was born in Egypt when the Israelites, God's people, were living in Egypt as slaves. Pharaoh, the new king of Egypt who did not know Joseph or his family, was afraid that because the Israelites were increasing in number, they could become mightier than the Egyptians and become a threat to his kingdom. This made him instruct all the midwives in Egypt to kill any male child born to the Israelites. However, the midwives feared God and they did not do what Pharaoh had asked them to do. Instead, they saved every male child that was born.

Moses was born during the period Pharaoh wanted the baby boys of the Israelites killed. Moses' mother, Jochebed, had to hide her baby. She hid him till he was three months old until she could not hide him any longer. Jochebed could not bear the thought of her baby being killed. She and Miriam, Moses' elder sister,

had to come up with a clever plan. They laid and secured Moses in a basket, leaving the basket to float on the River Nile. Miriam watched the basket from afar because she wanted to know what would happen to Moses.
She must have felt so nervous watching her baby brother float away, but she had to be brave, hoping God will protect him.

Soon after, Pharaoh's daughter came to the river with her maidens to bathe when she saw an ark-like basket floating on the river. She sent one of her maidens to get it. When Pharaoh's daughter opened it, she saw and heard baby Moses crying and she had compassion on him. She knew he must have been one of the Hebrew babies.

Miriam was courageous and remembered the clever plan she had with her mother before they set out to the River Nile. While Pharaoh's daughter stared at baby Moses with compassion, Miriam boldly walked up to the princess. She understood how important it was for her brother to stay alive and be nursed in the right environment. She was confident and asked Pharaoh's daughter an intelligent question, "Should I go and call one of the Hebrew women to nurse the child for you?"

"Yes", the princess replied.

Pharaoh's daughter must have thought to herself that Miriam was an intelligent young girl. Miriam went to fetch her mother right away. Because of Miriam's actions, Moses was nursed by his own mother, Jechobed, who even got paid by Pharaoh's daughter to take care of him until he was old enough to be taken to the palace.

God had a divine plan in place because Moses was the chosen one to deliver his people, the Israelites from Egypt.

Miriam grew to become a leader and a Prophetess to the Israelites. This made her a spokesperson for God. She also sang beautifully and led the people in music and dance.

Further reading; Exodus 2,15:20-21 & Numbers 20:1.

☀ Highlights

RELIABLE AND TRUSTWORTHY - Miriam was trustworthy. She had a great plan with her mum before they left home for the river and she stayed through to the plan. She did not come up with any contrary idea. Her mother could trust her to work with the plan. Pharaoh's daughter could also trust her. She was a leader and prophetess to the people of Israel and they also trusted her.

You too can be trustworthy. Trust is built when you start with the small things and step into the bigger things. Although you may make mistakes, always aim to be a person people can trust and depend on.

COURAGEOUS - Miriam showed amazing courage when she approached Pharaoh's daughter and asked if she could find a nurse for Moses. She also used her gifts boldly as a Prophetess and Minister of songs when she led the Israelites.

You need to be bold and live a fearless life because fear can hinder or limit a person from using their gifts and talents. God has not given you the spirit of fear but of power, of love and a sound mind.

CARING - Miriam was thoughtful and protective of her baby brother, Moses. She stood by the river, wondering what would happen to him.

You should also be kindhearted and sincerely want the best for not just your siblings, but for others too. Jesus gave us a new command to love each other just as Christ loved us.

CONFIDENT - Miriam spoke confidently as a young girl, and her confidence made Pharaoh's daughter know that the young girl knew exactly what she was saying and could be trusted. As a Prophetess, she led and sang with so much confidence that the Israelites were inspired to join her.

True confidence comes from within you, knowing who you are — and not from other people's opinions of you. God made you, so you should see yourself through his eyes. You are the apple of God's eyes! Do you know what God thinks about you?

Ponder

- Who does God say I am?

- Do I have any great ideas that I would like to share with my parents or caregivers, that can support and contribute to achieving my family's visions and goals?

- Am I loving and caring towards others?

- Am I too young to be bold and courageous?

- Am I trustworthy? Can people rely on me?

Declare

- I have faith in God and my faith in God increases.

- I am wise and I make wise decisions at all times.

- I am bold and courageous.

- Lord help me love others just as you love me.

- I am blessed. I trust in God and my confidence is in him.

MY NOTES

MY NOTES

SAMUEL

Samuel was born to his parents, Hannah and Elkanah. Before he was born, his mother, Hannah, was childless, and it made her sad and miserable. One day, after eating and drinking with her husband at a place called Shiloh, Hannah quietly got up and went to pray to the Lord. She cried, poured out her soul to God and made a special promise to God, "Lord All-Powerful, you can see how sad I am. Remember me. Don't forget me. If you will give me a son, I will give him to you. He will be yours his whole life, and as a Nazirite, he will not drink wine or strong drink, and no one will ever cut his hair."

That day, Eli the Priest of the temple was sitting at the doorpost of the temple. He watched Hannah as she wept. He saw her lips moving, but could not hear her voice, so he thought she was drunk. He approached her and asked her if she was drunk.

Hannah replied, "Sir, I have not drunk any wine or beer.

I am deeply troubled, and I was telling the Lord about all my problems. Don't think I am a bad woman. I have been praying for so long because I have so many troubles and I am very sad."

Eli spoke, "Go in peace. May the God of Israel give you what you asked for."

Hannah said, "May you be happy with me."

She left and had something to eat. She was not sad anymore. After this, God blessed Elkanah and Hannah with a son.

"His name is Samuel because I asked the Lord for him," Hannah said.

His mother weaned him and when the boy was old enough to eat solid food, Hannah took him to the Lord's house at Shiloh. She also took a bull that was three years old, twenty pounds of flour, and a bottle of wine. Hannah dedicated Samuel to the Lord and she said to Eli, the Priest, "I prayed for this child, and the Lord answered my prayer. He gave me this child. And now I give this child to the Lord. He will serve the Lord all his life." She did just as she had promised God.

Hannah left the boy there and worshipped the Lord.

Eli the Priest had two sons called Hophni and Phinehas.

They were both Priests like their father but they were evil men who did not care about the Lord. They did not care about how priests were supposed to treat people, nor did they respect the offerings made to the Lord. This was a terrible sin against the Lord.

Samuel however served the Lord even as a child. He was like a little helper in the temple who wore the linen ephod. Every year, Samuel's mother made a little robe for her son which she took to him when she went up to Shiloh with her husband for the sacrifice every year.

Eli blessed Elkanah and his wife, "May the Lord give you more children through Hannah who will take the place of Samuel, the boy she prayed for and gave to the Lord."

The Lord was kind to Hannah, and she had three more sons and two daughters. Meanwhile, Samuel grew up in the presence of the Lord and was Eli's helper. He served the Lord with him.

Back in those days, the Lord did not speak directly to people very often. He often spoke through Priests. Only a few people had visions. On a fateful night, the special lamp in the Lord's temple was still burning, so Samuel decided to lay down in the temple near where the Holy Box, the ark of God was kept. Samuel heard a voice call him and he answered, "Here I am."

He ran to meet Eli because he thought it was the Priest

that called him, "Here I am. You called me."

But Eli said, "I didn't call you. Go back to bed."

So Samuel went back to bed. Again the voice called, "Samuel!" Samuel ran back to Eli and said, "Here I am. You called me."

Eli said, "I did not call you. Go back to bed."

The voice that was calling out to Samuel was the voice of God but Samuel did not recognise the Lord because God had never spoken directly to him before.

The Lord called Samuel the third time. Again Samuel got up and went to Eli and said, "Here I am. You called me."

Finally, Eli understood that it must be the Lord who was calling the boy. He told Samuel, "Go to bed. If he calls you again, say, 'Speak, Lord. I am your servant, and I am listening.'"

So Samuel went back to bed. The Lord came and stood there. He called as he did before, saying, "Samuel, Samuel!"

This time, Samuel replied, "Speak. I am your servant, and I am listening."

The Lord began to speak to Samuel, "I will soon do things in Israel that will shock anyone who hears about them. I will do everything I said I would do against Eli and his family, everything from the beginning to the end. I told Eli I would punish his family forever. I will do this because Eli knew his two sons Phinehas and Hophni were saying and doing bad things against God. But he failed to control them. That is why I swore an oath that sacrifices and offerings will never take away the sins of the people in Eli's family."

Samuel lay down in bed until the morning came. He got up early and opened the doors of the Lord's house. He was afraid to tell Eli about the vision, but Eli Insisted on knowing, "What did God say to you? Don't hide it from me. God will punish you if you hide anything from the message he spoke to you."

So Samuel told Eli everything and hid nothing from him.

"He is the Lord. Let him do whatever he thinks is right," the Priest said.

The Lord was with Samuel while he grew up. He made sure all of Samuel's messages came true, and none could be said to be false. All of Israel knew that Samuel was a true prophet of the Lord.

The Lord continued to appear to Samuel at Shiloh.

There he told Samuel what he wanted.

Samuel judged Israel, God's own people, all the days of his life. He was Israel's last judge, and he went on to anoint Saul as king and eventually, David as king when God told him to do so.

Further reading; I Samuel 1-3.

☀ Highlights

CONSECRATED & DEDICATED - Samuel had a different childhood because before he was conceived, God had a plan for him, which he fulfilled.
Likewise, God has a plan for you too. Even before you were born. So you need to ensure you live a life set apart for Him. God wants us to be holy!

FOCUSED - Eli's two sons Phinehas and Hophni were Priests but they misbehaved and weren't good role models for Samuel to follow. With God's help, Samuel remained focused on serving and he was not distracted. We live in an imperfect world with imperfect families. However, remember you have to choose to be and remain focused always.

HUMBLE - Samuel was very humble and this character helped him serve and learn from Eli the Priest. When he was older, he was able to serve God and the people of Israel as a Judge, Priest and Prophet.
A humble person is wise. God wants us, his children, to be humble and teachable. We need to be ready to learn at all times because He hates pride.

OBEDIENT & DEVOTED - Eli taught Samuel how to hear God's voice. He did not just listen, but he obeyed and did as God told him to do. Because of his obedience, he became one of Israel's greatest judges.

In those times, the judges were both religious and political leaders. They were God's spokesmen to his people. As you yearn and learn to hear God's voice, please obey Him and do what He tells you to do. Remember everything God tells us to do is good and perfect. There is no confusion about it.

Ponder

- Am I too young to be devoted to the Lord? Am I too young to answer God's call on my life?

- Am I focused? What gets me distracted?

- What does it mean to be humble? Am I humble?

- Am I obedient to God and to higher authorities?

Declare

- Lord, I give You my life and I choose to live for you all the days of my life.

- I am a child of God and I hear His voice clearly, I am not confused.

- I have the courage to trust and obey God at all times.

- I am focused on who God made me and what He has called me to do.

MY NOTES

MY NOTES

DAVID

God made Saul the King of Israel. It was Samuel that anointed him. However, King Saul disobeyed God and God decided to choose a new king. Samuel felt sad about the rejection of Saul as the king of Israel, but God told Samuel to stop feeling sad, "I have rejected him as the king of Israel, fill your horn with olive oil and go to the house of a man called Jesse in Bethlehem as I have chosen one of his sons to be my king."

Samuel followed the strategy God gave him and did what God told him to do. He took a young calf with him to offer as sacrifice to the Lord in Bethlehem. When he entered the town, he invited the leaders as well as Jesse and his sons to take part in offering the sacrifice.

Jesse had eight sons, but he arrived at the gathering with seven sons. Samuel's thought when he saw Jesse's first son, Eliab, was that he had to be the one the Lord had chosen because he was tall and handsome but God told Samuel that he was not the chosen king.

God is more concerned with the heart of a person, and does not judge a person based on what they look like. This is what people do, but not God. Jesse sent his sons Abinadab, Shammah and his remaining four sons to Samuel but God had not chosen them.

So Samuel asked Jesse, "Do you have any other sons?"

"Yes," Jesse answered. "My youngest son David is out taking care of the sheep."

"Send for him, bring him here. We won't sit down until he arrives."

Jesse's youngest son soon arrived. David was ruddy, handsome and had bright eyes. Once Samuel saw him, God said to Samuel, "Get up and anoint him, he is the one I have chosen."

Samuel took the horn of olive oil and anointed David before his brothers and the Spirit of God came upon him from that day onwards.

The Spirit of God left King Saul and an evil spirit troubled Saul. Because of how much the evil spirit troubled him, Saul told his servants to find someone who played music well and bring such a person before him. One of his servants reported to him, "I have seen the son of a man called Jesse who lives in Bethlehem. He is talented in playing the harp. He is smart, brave and handsome, and God is with him."

King Saul sent a message through his servants to Jesse. The son of Jesse whom Saul requested turned out to be David and he was invited to the palace to play his harp for the king. Any time the evil spirit troubled Saul, David would play his harp and the evil spirit would leave Saul and he would begin to feel better. David was talented and King Saul loved him dearly. With Jesse's permission, David became the king's armour-bearer.

David was also a teenage shepherd boy. He spent most of his time in Bethlehem tending to his father's sheep in the wilderness and honing his skills on playing the harp. There were times while he was taking care of his father's sheep, wild animals came to attack some sheep in the flock. He was brave enough to chase and beat the wild animals until he rescued the sheep. One time, it was a lion and another time, a bear, that attacked his father's flock. David recovered the sheep from the mouth of wild animals. When the wild animals jumped on David, he caught them by their fur under their mouths and he hit them till he killed them. David killed both lion and bear.

When Saul was still king, the Philistines gathered their

armies for war to fight the armies of Israel. Their army camp was between Socoh and Azekah, at a town called Ephes Dammim. King Saul and the Israelite soldiers also gathered together and their army camp was in the Valley of Elah. The Philistines were on one hill, and the Israelites were on another hill with only a valley between them.

Saul's soldiers were lined up and ready to fight the Philistines. The Philistines were also ready to fight. The Philistine army had a champion fighter called Goliath. He was from Gath. He was over nine feet tall — a real life giant. He had a bronze helmet on his head and armour to protect his chest and legs. His armour was made of bronze and the chest armour weighed about one hundred and twenty five pounds. Goliath also had a bronze sword tied to his back. The wooden part of his spear was so big, that the iron spearhead weighed fifteen pounds.

Goliath had a soldier that always walked in front of him and helped him carry his shield. Every morning and evening for forty days, Goliath would come out of the Philistine camp, shouting and threatening to destroy Israel's whole army. He challenged Israel's army to choose someone to fight for them; if Israel's champion could kill him, then the philistines would be their slaves. If Goliath killed him, then the Israelites would serve them. When King Saul and his troop of soldiers heard what Goliath said, they were frightened.

Jesse's three oldest sons; Eliab, Abinadab and Shammah, were sent to King Saul as soldiers in his army. One day, Jesse sent David to check how his older brothers were doing and take some food supplies to them in the valley of Elah. David woke up early in the morning, left the sheep with another shepherd and took a basket of cooked grain and ten loaves of bread to his brothers in the army camp. He also took ten pieces of cheese for the officer who commanded his brothers' group of one thousand soldiers. When he got to the Israelites army camp, he left the things his father gave him with the supply keeper and ran off to greet his elder brothers. While he talked with them, Goliath the giant came out of the camp of the Philistines, shouting and boasting as he normally did to the army of Israel, and as usual, the Israelite soldiers were afraid and ran off. David heard all Goliath said and asked the soldiers that stood near him what the reward for killing the Philistine and taking away this insult from Israel was.

He was furious, "Who does Goliath think he is? And why does he think he can attack the army of the living God?"

The soldiers told David the reward for killing Goliath was a lot of money from King Saul, a daughter of the king as his wife and such a man's family would be free from paying taxes in Israel.

David's oldest brother, Eliab, heard him speaking to the

men and he was angry, "What are you doing here? Who did you leave the sheep with to come here to watch the battle?"

David replied, "What have I done? I did nothing wrong! I was only asking questions."

He left his brother and walked over to other soldiers asking the same question about the reward for defeating the giant. Some soldiers told the King about David and the question he was asking, and Saul sent for him.
When David was brought before King Saul, he spoke, "Let no man be discouraged. I will go and fight this giant, the Philistine."

Saul replied, "David, you do not stand a chance because you are a young boy and Goliath has been a soldier since he was a young boy."

David told the king about his bravery and how he had killed the lion and bear that attacked his father's sheep while he took care of them, "The same God that saved me from the lion and the bear, will also save me from this Philistine giant."

"Go and fight him and may the Lord God help you," Saul replied. He put David in his military uniform — a bronze helmet on David's head and armour on his body. David put on the sword and tried to walk around but he could not because he was not used to how heavy it was.

"I cannot fight with these things, because I have not trained with them," David told the king, and took them all off.

He walked to the brook and with his staff in his hand, he chose five smooth stones from the brook. He put them in his shepherd's bag, took his sling in his hand, and approached the Philistine giant. Goliath looked at David in disdain.

1 Samuel 17

43 Goliath said to David, "What is that stick for? Did you come to chase me away like a dog?" Then Goliath used the names of his gods to say curses against David. 44 He said to David, "Come here, and I'll feed your body to the birds and wild animals."

45 David said to the Philistine, "You come to me using sword, spear, and javelin. But I come to you in the name of the Lord All-Powerful, the God of the armies of Israel. You have said bad things about him.

46 Today the Lord will let me defeat you. I will kill you. I will cut off your head and feed your body to the birds and wild animals. And we will do the same thing to all the other Philistines too. Then all the world will know there is a God in Israel.

47 All the people gathered here will know that the Lord doesn't need swords or spears to save people. The battle belongs to the Lord, and he will help us defeat all of you."

Goliath began to approach David, and David ran towards him. David took a stone from his bag, put it in his sling and swung it at Goliath. The stone hit the middle of Goliath's forehead and he fell facedown to the ground. David killed Goliath with just a stone and a sling. He used Goliath's own sword to cut off his head.

When the Philistines saw that their champion was dead, they began to run away but the soldiers of Judah and Israel pursued them. They killed many Philistines and plundered their camp. David presented Goliath's head to King Saul and from that day, Saul had a bit of fear for David.

Saul saw that God had departed from him but was with David and made him successful. His fear and hatred for David grew. He decided to keep a close eye on him. Saul tried to kill him a few times, so David had to run to protect his life. He had different hideouts — caves, on the hills, the desert and more places — where he hid with his men. On two different occasions, David came close enough to Saul and had the opportunity to kill the king but he did not do so because he feared God.

David was thirty years old when he became king in Hebron, and he reigned over Judah for seven years and six months. When Saul died, David was crowned king in Jerusalem, he reigned over all of Israel and Judah as king for thirty three years. He was a king for a total of forty years. He had many sons and a daughter. He died at about 70 years old and his son Solomon became king.

David was a man after God's heart. He never lost a battle because God was with him. He respected and reverenced God. He wrote many of the Psalms recorded in the bible. He had a deep relationship with God and asked God for answers before making any decision. If he wanted to move to a different location to live, he asked God where to live. If he had to go to battle, he asked God first on whether or not to go and God always gave him a plan of action.

Further reading; I Samuel 16, 17, 18, 2 Samuel 5, Psalm 27, 51, 69.

☀ Highlights

WISE - David was a teenager when he was first introduced in the bible. He was too young to go to war and was focused on tending to his father's sheep. Although he was young, he feared God and made the right decisions.
The fear of God is the beginning of wisdom! This does not mean that you should be afraid of God. Having the fear of God means that you revere him and you have true respect and admiration for him. When you read the Psalms David wrote, it is clear that he truly revered and worshipped God while making his decisions. When you fear God, he shows you the best steps to take.

DEVOUT & GOD FEARING- David had a heart fully devoted to God, he worshipped God with his whole heart. He was called a man after God's own heart. David was imperfect like every human being but whenever he offended God, he repented wholeheartedly. He confessed any mistakes or sins he committed and he repented because he always felt so sorry.
God wants us to serve Him wholeheartedly. The first and greatest commandment is to love God with all our heart, soul and mind.

EXCELLENT & TENACIOUS - David was seen as the lamp of Israel. He was an extraordinary man. You would think, why was it not easy for David to ascend the throne despite being anointed by Samuel as king when he was a teenager? Why did he have to hide from Saul, to protect his life, even when he did nothing but succeed and excel?

What you have to realise is that sometimes, in order for you to ascend your throne and reign in what God has called you to be, you have to fight to break free of anything holding you back such as addictions, negative thoughts and emotions, or unhealthy habits. This is not a physical fight — you have to contend to maintain godly values and healthy boundaries. Sometimes, you can do this yourself but other times, you may need the help and support of a trustworthy person like a parent, guardian, counsellor, spiritual authority/leader, teacher or a mentor.

COURAGEOUS - Have you thought about how David, a teenager, could be so bold and fearless to confront Goliath, a giant philistine and war hero? He could not even wear Saul's army costume to go before Goliath because it was too heavy for him.

There is nothing like an easy or challenge-free life. The scriptures explain that in this world, you will have troubles but take courage, take heart because in Christ, you have overcome the world. You need to be courageous to face whatever challenge comes your way. If you feel discouraged, reflect and write down what may be causing your discouragement. Discuss it and sort it out. If you need to, reach out for help. Ask for advice, talk to God about it. Just don't give up!

PATIENCE - David was anointed king by Samuel as a teenager but he did not become king immediately. His journey to the throne took about fifteen years. God allowed David to go through the entire process because he needed the entire experience to lead God's people. God takes his time to build and mould an individual. There are several valuable lessons to learn in the process.

Are you facing any challenges? God sees them all. Talk to Him about it and learn through the process. God's grace is sufficient for you. His power is made perfect in your weakness.

MEDITATION & SOLITUDE - David wrote many books of Psalms because of his ability to meditate and reflect on the goodness of God in both the good times and challenging times in his life. You can train yourself to meditate and not worry. Meditate on a verse a day, a bible story, or a bible character and reflect on ways you can apply what you have learned in your life and make a difference.

David spent years in the wilderness. These were not fun times for him. As a shepherd boy, there were times he was alone in the desert with the sheep. While he was alone, he must have learned how to play and sharpen his skills on the harp. David was poetic with a vast imagination. Some of the Psalms he wrote suggest that he may have discovered and developed these attributes in the quietness of the wilderness.

There is power in silence. Sometimes, it is during the silence you can meditate, reflect, and reassess your journey in life so that you can map out how to move forward.

If you fill all of your time with several activities because you are bored, your productivity would be affected. Plan to have a quiet time every day. Such a time is not a boring moment. Use this time positively. Pray during your quiet moments, reflect and meditate. While meditating, your thoughts should be positive and not be filled with worry.

Meditate on a verse or passage. You can start by dedicating five or ten minutes to your quiet time daily, and after a while keep growing and increasing the time frame. Plan quiet moments, to develop your gifts and improve your talents. Do not spend all your free time on social media or gaming. Remember, solitude improves your creativity, it helps you concentrate better and discover yourself.

SUCCESS- David had good success because he asked God before making decisions in his life — whether to go to battle or not, where to live and many more aspects of his life. Because he always asked God, he was given directions and a master plan to live by, and God's plan can never fail. David was a skilled warrior and a hero but he chose to use his skill to please, honour, and obey God. This made God's favour to be upon him.

What are your gifts and talents? What are you skilled in? Is it in music, drama, writing, painting, sports, or craftwork and so on? Whatever it may be, it is not too little or too grand to serve God with. When you discover your talents, develop and deploy them to honour God. Share your plans with the Lord, and you will succeed.

Ponder

- What does 'the fear of God mean' to me? Do you fear God?

- Are you facing any challenges? In what ways are you managing them?

- Are you patient? In what ways can you be more patient and enduring?

- Do you know what your talents and gifts are? In what ways can you develop and use them for God's Glory?

🗣 Declare

- I give you my plans Lord and I trust You to direct my path.

- I am not afraid, I am strong and courageous because God holds me. He goes with me. He will not leave nor abandon me.

- Lord help me to always meditate on your word and do all you say. Thank you Lord for making me prosperous. I have good success.

- In whatever I do, I do it all to the glory of God.

- God is my light and my salvation. I am not afraid because he is my defence.

MY NOTES

MY NOTES

KING JEHOASH / JOASH

Joash became king when he was seven years old. His mother was Zibiah of Beersheba and his father was King Ahaziah, the wicked king. When the king was killed, Athaliah, the mother of King Ahaziah, murdered all the sons of the king — her own grandchildren and royal heirs to the throne in Judah. Joash was only a baby then and he was stolen away from the king's sons so that he would not be killed like his brothers. His aunt, Jehosheba, hid him and kept him safe from his wicked grandmother. Jehosheba was King Jehoram's daughter, the sister of King Ahaziah and the wife of Jehoiada. Jehosheba and her husband, Jehoiada the Priest, hid Joash and his nurse with the priests in the inside bedroom of God's Temple for six years. During that time, Athaliah ruled over the land of Judah as queen.

Seven years later, Jehoiada showed his strength and made an agreement with five army captains. These captains were Azariah son of Jeroham, Ishmael son of

Jehohanan, Azariah son of Obed, Maaseiah son of Adaiah, and Elishaphat son of Zicri. These men secretly went around Judah and gathered the Levites from all the towns of Judah. They also gathered the leaders of the families of Israel. They all had a meeting in the temple in Jerusalem. There in the Temple of the Lord, Jehoiada showed them the king's son, and all the people in the meeting made an agreement with the young king. Jehoiada said to the people, "The king's son will rule". That is what the Lord promised about David's descendants.

Jehoiada then went ahead to give the men commands and instructions on the positions they were to take at the palace, the gate and the temple, in preparation of their plans to dethrone Athalia and crown the king's young son He did not excuse any priest or captain from his commands — it included those on and off duty. Jehoiada gave spears and large and small shields that belonged to King David to the officers. The weapons had been kept in God's Temple. They were to stand in the positions he had assigned to them with a weapon in every man's hand. They obeyed everything Jehoiada the priest told them to do. The men stood all the way from the right side of the Temple to the left side of the Temple. Some stood near the altar, and some, near the king. These men brought out Joash, they put the crown on his head and gave him a copy of God's laws. Then they made Joash the new king. Jehoiada and his sons anointed Joash and said, "Long live the king!" Everyone clapped their hands and shouted, "Long live the king!" Queen Athaliah heard the noise of the people running to the Temple and praising the king. She went into the Lord's Temple to see what the people were so excited about. She looked and saw the young king standing by his column at the front entrance. The officers and the men who blew trumpets stood near the king. The people of the land were happy and blowing trumpets. The singers were playing instruments of music. They led the people in singing praises. Then Athaliah tore her clothes and cried out, "Treason! Treason!"

Jehoiada the priest gave a command to the captains who were in charge of the soldiers, "Take Athaliah outside of the Temple area. Kill any of her followers, but do not kill them in the Lord's Temple." The soldiers grabbed Athaliah and killed her as soon as she went through the horse's gate, an entrance to the king's palace.

Then Jehoiada made an agreement between the Lord, the king and the people. This agreement showed that the king and the people belonged to the Lord. All the people went into the temple of the idol Baal and tore it down. They demolished the altars and idols that were in Baal's temple and killed Mattan the priest of Baal in front of the altars of Baal.

After all this, Jehoiada chose Levites as the priests to be

responsible for the Lord's Temple because the former king, David had given the Levites the job of being responsible for the Lord's temple. They were to offer burnt offerings to the Lord the way the Law of Moses commanded. They offered the sacrifices with much joy and singing the way David commanded. Jehoiada put guards at the gates of the Lord's Temple to prevent any unclean person from entering the Temple.

Jehoiada with the army captains, the leaders, the rulers of the people, and all the people of the land followed the king and left the temple. They went through the Upper Gate to the king's palace and put the king on the throne. The people of Judah were happy, and the city of Jerusalem had peace because the wicked queen, Athaliah, had been killed with a sword.

Joash was seven years old when he became king and he ruled for forty years in Jerusalem. Jehoiada got him married and he had sons and daughters. For as long as Jehoiada lived, Joash did what the Lord considered right. He did what Jehoiada the priest taught him.

When Joash was in his early twenties, he decided to rebuild the Lord's Temple. Joash called the priests and the Levites together. He said to them, "Go out to the towns of Judah and gather the money all the Israelites pay every year in tax. Use that money to rebuild your God's Temple. Hurry and do this." However, the Levites did not hurry.

So King Joash called Jehoiada, the leading priest, "Jehoiada, why haven't you made the Levites bring in the tax money from Judah and Jerusalem? Moses, the Lord's servant, and the Israelites used that tax money for the Tent of the Agreement."

King Joash gave a command for a box to be made and put outside the gate at the Lord's Temple. The Levites then made an announcement in Judah and Jerusalem. They told the people to bring in their tax money for the Lord. That tax money is what Moses, the servant of God, had required the Israelites to give while they were in the desert. All the leaders and the people were happy. They brought their money and put it in the box. They continued giving until the box was full. Every time the box got filled up, the Levites would take the box to the king's officials. The king's secretary and the leading priest's officer would take the money out of the box and ask for the box to be returned. They did this often and gathered a lot of money.

King Joash and Jehoiada gave the money to the people who worked on the Lord's Temple. The people who worked on the Lord's Temple hired skilled woodcarvers and carpenters as well as workers who knew how to work with iron and bronze to rebuild the Lord's Temple. The men who supervised the work were very faithful and could be trusted. The rebuilding of the

Temple was successful. The temple was made even stronger. When the workers finished, they brought the money that was left to King Joash and Jehoiada. They used that money to make things used for burnt offerings and the service in the Temple. They also made bowls and other things from gold and silver. The priests offered burnt offerings in the Lord's Temple every day while Jehoiada was alive.

Jehoiada lived a very long life and died when he was 130 years old. The people buried Jehoiada in the City of David where the kings were buried. The people buried Jehoiada there because in his life he did a lot of good in Israel for God and for God's Temple.

After Jehoiada died, the leaders of Judah came and bowed to King Joash. They persuaded the king to listen to their advice. They all stopped worshipping at the Temple of the Lord, the God their ancestors worshipped. Instead, they started worshipping Asherah poles and other idols like wooden images and idols. Because they sinned in this way, God was angry with the people of Judah and Jerusalem. God sent prophets to the people to instruct them to turn away from idolatry and to come back to the Lord. The prophets warned the people, but they refused to listen.

The Spirit of God filled Zechariah the son of Jehoiada the priest, and one day, he stood in front of the people and said, "This is what God says: 'Why do you people refuse to obey the Lord's commands? You will not be successful. You have left the Lord. So he has also left you!"

The leaders were angry and made evil plans against Zechariah. The king commanded the people to kill Zechariah, so they threw rocks at him in the courtyard of the Lord's temple until he was dead. King Joash did not remember that Zechariah's father, Jehoiada, was kind to him. Before Zechariah died, he said, "May the Lord see what you are doing and punish you!"

At the end of the year, the Syrian army came against Joash. They attacked Judah and Jerusalem and killed all the leaders of the people. They sent all the valuable things to the king of Damascus. The Syrian army came with only a small group of men, but the Lord let them defeat the much larger army of Judah. This was punishment for Joash and the people for leaving the Lord and worshipping idols. When the Syrians left, Joash was badly wounded. His own servants made evil plans against him. They did this because Joash had killed Zechariah. The servants killed Joash on his own bed. After he died, the people buried him in the City of David, but not in the place where the kings were buried. Joash's son Amaziah, became the new king after him.

Further reading; 2 Kings 11, 12 and 13. 2 Chronicles 22:10-12, 23 and 24. 1 Corinthians 15:33, 1 Corinthians 6:19.

☀ Highlights

HIS CALL - God used Jehosheba to save Joash and ensure he received his inheritance as king. His age did not hinder God's plan. God will do whatever it takes to ensure you are preserved to fulfil your call regardless of your age.
Your age cannot restrict God from using you to fulfil his plans and purpose for your life.

HIS MENTOR - Jehoiada the priest was a great mentor to Joash. He taught him God's way and Joash did right before God. Jehoiada gave him guidance, advised him as a father and as a leader.
Who you choose to mentor you in any area is very important. They influence what you learn, your opinions and your perspective on life. Mentors guide you to make the right and wise decisions in various situations. So choose your mentors wisely.

HIS WORK - King Joash did a great job rebuilding the temple especially because the building was old, needed a lot of repairs and was neglected by the previous evil rulers. His fundraising for the temple project was so effective that everyone was a part of it.
The bible says our body is the temple of the Holy Spirit that lives inside of us, given by God. You have to look after your body — what you eat and drink is important, even how you dress too. Take time to rest.
Also, find different ways to look after God's house —

the physical church building. Every one of us has to ensure it is well maintained.

HIS CHOICES - He made some wise choices when his mentor Jehoiada the priest was alive but sadly after he died Joash made wrong choices. It was ironic because he was older and not a child king anymore.
Every day of your life, you will make choices. It is important you make wise choices no matter how trivial any situation seems. Ask God to help you get it right. Also, train and discipline yourself to get it right.

HIS COMPANY- When King Joash was in great company, he did great things and made good choices. After Jehoiada the priest died, the people around him were bad company. They gave him bad advice and had a negative influence on him. He had the option of having Zechariah the priest in his company of advisers but instead, he refused to listen to his advice from God and he killed him.
Be careful of the friends you make, especially the ones you keep close to you and the ones you choose to learn from because bad company corrupts good character.

HIS INGRATITUDE - He forgot how God used Jehoiada and his wife to spare him as an infant and protect him from his wicked grandmother who killed his other siblings. He forgot how kind and good Jehoiada was to him and killed his son Zechariah. Live daily in gratitude, always look for things and people to be grateful for. We should give God thanks in all things.

HIS GROWTH - Although King Joash was taught in the ways of God by Jehoiada and did what was right, he did not grow into the ways of the Lord. He had a great privilege but he did not understand the value of the godly counsel he had in leadership.
Not everyone has the privilege of having such godly counsel. Be thankful however for what you have and what you get to learn while reading this book. Be prepared to develop yourself to be the best with what you learn. Maturity is your responsibility.

IDOLATRY - Unfortunately King Joash went into the worship of false gods because he lost his faith in God. This is the worship of someone or something as if they were God. Sometimes an idol can be those things that keep you away from loving, worshipping and serving God with all your heart. God wants us all to worship Him in spirit and truth, with our whole heart.

Ponder

- Am I too young to lead?

- Who are my friends and who is my mentor? Who do I listen to and where do I get godly advice from?

- In what different ways can I grow and develop to be the best version of myself?

🗣 Declare

- I am saved to be all God has made and called me to be.

- I am discerning — I keep and walk in good company.

- Lord show me my mentor(s) and help me choose my friends.

- I receive wise counsel and I thrive with it.

MY NOTES

MY NOTES

KING AZARIAH / UZZIAH

After King Amaziah died and was buried with his ancestors, the people of Judah chose Uzziah to be the new king. Amaziah was Uzziah's father and his mother's name was Jecoliah. Jecoliah was from Jerusalem. Uzziah who is also known as Azariah was sixteen years old when he became king and he ruled for fifty-two years in Jerusalem. He rebuilt the town of Elath and gave it back to Judah. However, he did not destroy the high places. Some people still made sacrifices and burned incense in these places of worship.

Uzziah did what God wanted him to do. He obeyed God just as his father, Amaziah had done. While Zechariah was alive, Uzziah followed God. Zechariah understood God's visions and he taught Uzziah how to respect and obey God. As long as King Uzziah obeyed God, God gave him good success.

King Uzziah fought a war against the Philistines. He

tore down the walls around the towns of Gath, Jabneh, and Ashdod. He built towns near the town of Ashdod and in other places among the Philistines. God helped Uzziah fight the Philistines, the Arabians living in the town of Gur Baal, and the Meunites. The Ammonites paid tribute to King Uzziah. He became very strong and powerful and his name became famous all the way to the border of Egypt.

Uzziah built towers in Jerusalem, at the Corner Gate, at the Valley Gate, and at the place where the wall turned. He made them strong and secure. He also built towers in the desert and dug many wells because he had a lot of cattle in the hill country and in the plains. He loved farming so he had farmers in the mountains and in the lands where the soil was good. He also had vinedressers — men who took care of vineyards.

King Uzziah had an army of trained soldiers. They were put in groups by Jeiel the secretary and Maaseiah the officer. Hananiah, one of the king's officers, was made their overall leader. There were 2600 chief officers that led all the soldiers and under them were an army of 307,500 men who fought with great power. These soldiers helped the king fight against the kingdom's enemy. Uzziah gave the army shields, spears, helmets, armour, bows, and stones for their slings. In Jerusalem, Uzziah got clever men to invent machines that could shoot arrows and large rocks. These machines were put on the towers and corner walls to shoot arrows and large rocks. These machines were put on the towers and corner walls to shoot arrows and large rocks. These feats made Uzziah even more famous and powerful.

King Uzziah soon became proud and stopped being faithful to God. He offended God by entering into the Lord's Temple to burn incense on the altar. Azariah the priest, and eighty other brave priests who served the Lord followed Uzziah into the Temple. They told him he was wrong, "Uzziah, it is not your job to burn incense to the Lord. It is not right! That job is for the priests, the sons of Aaron, as they are the only ones who have been prepared for the holy work of burning incense. You have not been faithful to God, so you must go out of the Most Holy Place. The Lord God will not honour you for this."

Uzziah became angry with the priests, and while he was displaying his anger, right before the priests, leprosy broke out on his forehead. The priests quickly forced him out of the Temple because he had become unclean. Uzziah knew the Lord had punished him, and he himself hurried out because he was ashamed.

Uzziah was a leper until the day he died. He had to live in a separate house. He could never enter the Lord's Temple again. His son Jotham controlled the king's palace and became governor — he judged the people. When Uzziah died, he was not buried with his ancestors. Rather, he was in a field close to where his ancestors were buried. This was because the people said, "Uzziah is a leper." Uzziah's son Jotham became the new king in his place.

Further reading; 2 Kings 15:1-6, 2 Chronicles 26, James 4:6, Deuteronomy 8:18, Psalm 18:32, Proverbs 16:18.

☀ Highlights

HUMILITY - King Uzziah started off as a young humble boy that had great respect for God and obeyed Him. He was willing to learn and grow as a leader and he worked closely with Zechariah the prophet to know God's will for the people he led.
God expects us all to be humble and remain humble as we grow older. God is against the proud, but He is kind to the humble.

SUCCESSFUL - King Uzziah had a relationship with God and was wealthy because God made him prosper. He was a rich king and lacked nothing — livestock, crops, vineyards, his huge army and his people. There was always plenty to eat and drink.
True wealth and riches come from God. He gives the power to get wealth. You need to carefully obey God's commands to be truly successful. However, true success is not only about material possessions.

STRENGTH- King Uzziah was strong and powerful. His army was strong and equipped and they won their battles because God was with them.
It is God that arms us with strength and makes our way perfect. With God's help, we can fight and defeat the attacks of Satan. Jesus has given you the authority and by His name, you have victory.

FAME - King Uzziah was wealthy, strong and he

became known far and wide because God was with him and blessed him.

In these times, there is a huge quest to be popular and famous but do not forget to ask yourself, "Why do I want fame?. When or if I become famous or an influencer will I bring others closer to God or take them away from God?" Remember in whatever you choose to be or do, you are God's ambassador on earth. Yes, you represent God!

PRIDE - King Uzziah became so proud that he forgot all his success came from God. He lost his mind by breaking God's laws and unfortunately it came with a punishment.

Pride comes before destruction. Regardless of how popular and successful you are, nothing should take God's place in your heart. God wants us to be humble people, he gives grace to the humble.

Ponder

- Am I a humble person?

- What do I want to be in the future and how would I use it to help others?

- Where does my strength lie? In what areas do I need to be stronger?

Declare

- I receive grace from God to be and remain humble all my life.

- I can do whatever I have to do because Christ is my strength.

- I do not have two masters, I serve God only.

MY NOTES

MY NOTES

KING MANASSEH

Manasseh was twelve years old when he became king of Judah. He reigned as king for fifty-five years in Jerusalem. His mother's name was Hephzibah while his father was Hezekiah. King Manasseh did many things that God said were wrong. He followed the terrible and sinful ways of the nations that the Lord had forced out of the land before the Israelites settled upon those lands. King Manasseh rebuilt the high places that his father Hezekiah destroyed. He also built altars for the Baal gods and made Asherah poles. Manasseh worshipped and served the stars of heaven. He even built altars for false gods in the Lord's own Temple.

King Manasseh also made a statue of an idol and put it in God's Temple — the very same Temple that God had talked about to David and his son Solomon. God had said, "I have chosen Jerusalem from all the cities in Israel. I will put my name in the Temple in Jerusalem forever. I will not cause the Israelites to leave the land that I gave to their ancestors. I will let the people stay in their land if they obey everything (all the laws and rules) I commanded them and all the teachings that my servant Moses gave them."

King Manasseh burned his own son for a sacrifice to the false gods he served in the Valley of Ben Hinnom. He also used magic by doing soothsaying, witchcraft(divination), and sorcery, trying to know the future. He visited and talked with mediums and wizards. He did many things that were evil before God and he made God angry.

Manasseh inspired the people of Judah and the people living in Jerusalem to do wrong and they were worse than the nations that were in the land before the Israelites — and the Lord destroyed those people.
God used his servants, the prophets, to speak to Manasseh and to his people, but they refused to listen. So God brought commanders from the Assyrian army, sent by the King of Assyria to attack Judah. These commanders captured King Manasseh and made him their prisoner. They put hooks on him and brass chains on his hands and took him to the country of Babylon. Because he was in so much trouble and suffering, Manasseh humbled himself before God. He prayed to God and begged for help. God heard his begging and felt sorry for him, so he let Manasseh return to Jerusalem and to his throne. This made King Manasseh

know that the Lord is the true God.

After that happened, Manasseh built a very high outer wall for the City of David. This wall went to the west of Gihon Spring in Kidron Valley, to the entrance of the Fish Gate, and around the hill of Ophel. Afterwards, he put officers in all the fortresses in Judah. Manasseh removed all the idols from the Lord's temple, brought down all the altars he built on the temple hill and across the city of Jerusalem, and threw all the strange idol gods out of Jerusalem.

King Manasseh repaired the Lord's altar and offered peace offerings and thank offerings on it. He gave a command that all the people of Judah should serve the Lord, the God of Israel. The people continued to offer sacrifices at the high places, but this time, their sacrifices were made only to the Lord their God and not any false idols.

When Manasseh died, the people buried him in his own palace — in the garden at his house. It was called the "Garden of Uzza". Manasseh's son, Amon became the new king after him.

Further reading; 2 Chronicles 33: 1- 20, 2 Kings 21:1-18.

☀ Highlights

SIN - King Manasseh was so wicked that he killed his own son. His love for himself and hatred for God led others to sin. He worshipped the stars and made statues to worship as his gods. His evil practices included soothsaying (fortune-telling), witchcraft, consulting spiritists and mediums because he wanted to know the future.

These acts are strictly forbidden by God. Although they may seem popular in books, on TV shows, and in games, God does not want us to practice these things because they get their fake powers from the devil. A person who serves God and has faith in Him should not be involved in evil practices like going to a fortune teller or consulting a witch. God expects His children to worship Him only in spirit and truth.

REPENTANCE - There are consequences for our actions and King Manasseh had to face his own consequences when he did not listen to God's warnings through the prophets. He realised he was wrong and living in sin, so he repented but that was after God allowed him to suffer as a prisoner. After he repented and begged God, God saw he was sincere and forgave him.

God gives us all another chance, His mercy and grace are available for all to receive. When you repent and change from wrongdoings, you do not just say 'I am sorry, Lord forgive me, but you should mean those words sincerely because He sees our hearts. Repentance goes beyond words, it shows in our actions.

RESTORATION - King Manasseh removed and destroyed all the idols he made in the land and turned away from all his evil practices. He went on to offer sacrifices to God Almighty and he turned his people back to God.

When you repent from your sins and say, "I am sorry. Lord please forgive me", God expects us to truly change from any wrongdoings. With the help of the Holy Spirit, we can be transformed but you need to ask for the help and believe God will change you.

Ponder

- Do you know God loves us so much that He sent Jesus Christ to die for our sins to give us hope and eternal life?

- Did you know that God's grace and mercy is available for you when you sincerely repent and turn from your wrongdoings?

- What do you do when you offend God?

Declare

- Lord, I am sorry for all my wrongdoings. Please have mercy and forgive me.

- Lord, I give You all my struggles and weaknesses and I ask the Holy Spirit to help me and transform me to be like Christ.

- I am forgiven and I accept God's unfailing love.

MY NOTES

MY NOTES

KING JOSIAH

Josiah was eight years old when he became king and he reigned for thirty-one years in Jerusalem. His mother's name was Jedidah. He lived in a way that pleased the Lord, always doing what was right, as his father David had done. Josiah was young — sixteen years old — when he began to follow and obey God. In his twelfth year as king, he started destroying the high places, the Asherah poles, and idols that were carved or made from moulds from Judah and Jerusalem. Under Josiah's supervision, the people broke down the altars for the Baal gods. He cut down the incense altars that stood high above the people. He beat the broken idols into powder and sprinkled the powder on the graves of the people who had offered sacrifices to the Baal gods. He even burned the bones of the priests who had served the Baal gods on their own altars. This was how he destroyed idols and idol worship in Judah and Jerusalem. Josiah also made sure idolatry was abolished from the towns in the areas of Manasseh, Ephraim, Simeon, and all the way to Naphtali. He did the same for the ruins near all these towns.

In Josiah's eighteenth year as king of Judah, he decided to clean up the land as well as the Temple of the Lord. In the past, the kings of Judah did not care that the Temple buildings had become old and ruined, but Josiah was different. He sent Shaphan, Maaseiah, and Joah to rebuild and repair the Temple. Shaphan was the son of Azaliah, Maaseiah was the city leader, and Joah was the son of Joahaz. He was also the recorder who wrote about what happened. King Josiah sent these men to Hilkiah the high priest and commanded that the Temple be repaired. They gave the priest the money that people had given for rebuilding God's Temple. The Levite doorkeepers had collected this money from the people of Manasseh, Ephraim, and from all the Israelites who were left. They also collected money from the people of Judah, the people of Benjamin and all the people living in Jerusalem. The Levites paid the men who supervised the work on the Lord's Temple and the supervisors in turn paid the workers who repaired the Lord's Temple. Carpenters and builders were given money to buy wood and large rocks that were already cut. The wood was used during rebuilding and to make beams for the buildings. The men worked faithfully and were supervised by Jahath and Obadiah. Jahath and Obadiah were Levites, and they were descendants of Merari. Other supervisors were Zechariah and Meshullam who were descendants of Kohath. The Levites who were skilled in playing instruments of music also supervised the labourers and other workers. Some Levites worked as secretaries (scribes), officials, and doorkeepers.

While working, the Levites brought out the money that was in the Lord's Temple, and Hilkiah the priest found the Book of the Law of the Lord that was given through Moses. Hilkiah said to Shaphan the secretary (scribe), "I found the Book of the Law in the Temple." Hilkiah gave the book to Shaphan and Shaphan took the holy book to King Josiah.
Shaphan reported back to the king, "Your servants are doing everything you told them to do. They collected the money that was in the Lord's Temple and are paying the supervisors and the workers." He continued, "Hilkiah the priest gave a book to me."

Shaphan then read some parts of the book to the king. When King Josiah heard the words of the law being read, he tore his clothes. He commanded Hilkiah the priest, Ahikam son of Shaphan, Abdon son of Micah, Shaphan the secretary (scribe), and Asaiah the servant of the king, "Go, ask the Lord for me and for the people who are left in Israel and in Judah. Ask about the words in the book that was found. The Lord is very angry with us because our ancestors did not obey the Lord's word. They did not do everything written in this book."

So Hilkiah and the other men the king sent went to Jerusalem to see Huldah the prophetess. She was the wife of Shallum, the son of Tokhath, whose father was Hasrah, keeper of the king's wardrobe. Hilkiah and the men sent by the king told Huldah what had happened.

Huldah said to them, "This is what the Lord, the God of

Israel, says: Tell the man who sent you — King Josiah — that the Lord says, 'I will bring trouble to this place and to the people living here. I will bring all the terrible things that are written in the book that was read before the king of Judah. I will do this because the people left me and burned incense to other gods. They made me angry because of all the bad things they have done. So I will pour out my anger on this place. Like a hot burning fire, my anger will not be put out!'

But to the King Josiah of Judah, who sent you to ask what the Lord wants. Tell him, This is what the Lord, the God of Israel, says about the words you heard being read: 'Josiah, when you heard my words against this city and its people, you were sorry and humbled yourself before me. You even tore your clothes to show your sorrow and cried before me. Because your heart was tender, I the Lord, have heard you. And I will take you to be with your fathers, you will go to your grave in peace. You will not have to see any of the trouble that I will bring on this place and on the people living here."

Hilkiah and the men the king sent brought back this message from the prophetess to King Josiah.

King Josiah called all the elders of Judah and Jerusalem to attend a meeting with him. He went up to the Lord's Temple and people from Judah, people living in Jerusalem, the priests, the Levites, and all the people both great and small, were with Josiah. He read the Book of the Agreement — the holy book that was found in the Lord's Temple to them. Afterwards, the king stood up and made an agreement with the Lord to follow and obey the Lord's commands, laws, and rules written in the holy book, with all his heart and soul. He made all the people of Jerusalem and Benjamin promise to accept the agreement. The people of Jerusalem obeyed the agreement.

Josiah destroyed all the terrible idols, mediums and the horrible things people worshipped in Judah, Jerusalem and the entire country of Israel. He made all the Israelites serve the Lord and as long as Josiah was alive, the people continued to serve the Lord, the God of their fathers.
King Josiah commanded and said to the people, "Celebrate the Passover for the Lord your God. Do this just as it is written in the Book of the Agreement."

In the eighteenth year of King Josiah's reign, they celebrated the Passover for the Lord in Jerusalem. The former Kings of Israel and Kings of Judah had never had such a big celebration for Passover. The people had not celebrated a Passover like that since the days when the judges ruled Israel.

There had never been a king like Josiah before. He turned to the Lord with all his heart, all his soul, and all his strength. No king had followed all the Laws of Moses like Josiah did and there was never another king like Josiah.
When King Josiah died in battle, the people of the land took Josiah's son Jehoahaz and anointed him as their new king.

Further reading; 2 Kings 22, 23:1-30, 2 Chronicles 34 & 35.

☀ Highlights

TENDER-HEARTED - A tenderhearted person lives a blessed life! When King Josiah heard the words of the scriptures read to him, he was so upset that he tore his clothes because the people had been living in disobedience and idolatry for a long time. God's commandments written in the holy book were not obeyed even by their forefathers and ancestors and it made him sad. God's word was important to King Josiah and he was humble enough to listen and obey it. This means he was a teachable person.

Having a teachable spirit puts you ahead in life because you learn daily through experiences and from others. Lifelong learners have a wide range of understanding. The scriptures, although written by men, were all inspired by God to teach, train, equip, instruct, correct and complete us for every good work. God's word is truth and when we read and study it, we are set free.

RESPONSIBLE - King Josiah took responsibility immediately for the actions of the people of Judah and how they failed to please God even though it was not intentional. He did not blame his forefathers for disobeying God, rather, he took action immediately to set things right, led the people to repent and plead for God's mercy on him and his people. He was a good leader and led by example. He cared about the fate of others. He sent his servants, including the priests and scribes to Huldah the prophetess to know what God was saying because he was interested in knowing what to do and how to get it right.

It is not enough to feel sorry and get emotional about God's word. There are actions that need to be taken. King Josiah involved the leaders of the land and the people and they made a commitment to be restored. You are responsible for a lot of the decisions you make for your life especially as you grow older. In some situations, instead of putting the blame on someone else when things don't work out, lean on God and ask for his mercy to help you live a better life.

RESTORATION & RESTITUTION - King Josiah cleansed his land of idolatry by destroying the shrines, mediums, their priests, the idols his predecessors the previous kings had built, and evil altars of false gods the people served. He destroyed everything God detested in the land of Judah and Jerusalem. He had his people celebrate Passover, a special feast in honour of God, which they had not celebrated for a while because they had evil kings. He made a huge impact and left a legacy in the records of the bible. There was no king before him that turned to the Lord with all his heart, with all his soul, and with all his might, according to all the law of Moses; neither did there arise any king like him.
Some decisions we make in life, good or bad, do not only affect us but others as well. Hence, we always have

to ensure that we make wise decisions. When you repent and make a decision to change, you have to consciously take action to get rid of whatever makes you make poor decisions. This may mean deciding not to go to certain places anymore, cutting off from some bad friends, not watching some programmes, or not reading certain books and magazines. Whatever it takes to be restored back to God's plan for you, do it. God's help is there for you.

Ponder

- How important is God's word to me and what do I do after studying God's word?

- Do I always look for who to blame or who is at fault, without accepting responsibility?

- When things are not going right with me or around me, do I look for solutions and ask God for help to get it right?

- What positive difference or impact am I making in my family, school, church, and community?

Declare

- I read and hear your word oh Lord. I love you and I obey your commands.

- Your word oh Lord is a lamp to my feet and a light

to my path.

- My heart is loyal to you Lord. Help me to always obey all your commands.

- I know what is right and I do it.

MY NOTES

MY NOTES

ELISHA AND THE YOUTH

The men of the city of Jericho met Elisha the Prophet of God and said to him, "Sir, you can see this city is in a nice place, but the water is bad and the land cannot grow crops."

Elisha replied, "Bring me a new bowl and put salt in it." They brought the bowl to Elisha and he took it to the place where the water was flowing from the ground. Elisha threw the salt into the water and said, "The Lord said, 'I am healing this water and making it pure! From now on this water will not cause any more death or keep the land from growing crops."

It happened just as Elisha said and the water was made pure.

Elisha left the city of Jericho on his way to Bethel. While he was walking up the road to the city, he came across some young boys that were coming out of the city. As soon as they saw him, they started making fun of him.

They chanted, "Go away, you bald-headed man! Go away, you bald-headed man!"

Elisha the Prophet turned around and saw the forty two boys making fun of him. He cursed them in the name of the Lord. He asked that bad things would happen to them. Two female bears suddenly came out of the woods and attacked the boys and all forty two boys were destroyed by the bears. Elisha left Bethel and went to Mount Carmel and from there he went back to Samaria.

Further reading; 2 Kings 2:19 - 25, 2 Chronicles 36:16, Psalm 105:15, 1 Timothy 5:17.

Highlights

- It is important to God that you honour and respect your elders, parents — both biological and spiritual parents — and those who have authority over you. God expects you to honour and not mock people he has put in authority over you. If they offend you, speak to them respectfully about it and resolve any differences. Involve another trusted person if there is a need to do so.

  1 Peter 2:17 Show respect for all people. Love your brothers and sisters in God's family. Respect God, and honour the king.

Ponder

- Who are those in authority over me?

- Who are my spiritual leaders?

- In what ways can I honour them?

Declare

- I honour all people and I give double honour to my elders. I respect everyone in authority over me.

MY NOTES

MY NOTES

NAAMAN'S SERVANT GIRL

Naaman was the captain of the Syrian army. He was a great man and very important to the king of Syria because the Lord used him to lead the land of Syria to victory in many battles. However, as powerful and great as Naaman was, he still suffered and was sick with leprosy.

Israel and Syria were not on friendly terms, and the Syrian army sent many groups of soldiers to raid and fight in Israel. On one of those raids, they took a little girl from the land of Israel and brought her back to Syria. The girl became a maidservant of Naaman's wife and served diligently. One day, she spoke to her mistress and said, "I wish that my master would meet the prophet who lives in Samaria. He could heal Naaman of his leprosy."

Naaman went to the king and told him what the Israelite girl said.

The king of Syria said, "Go now, and I will send a letter to the king of Israel.

Although the name of the servant girl was never mentioned in the bible, her faith and confidence spoke volumes as she made her master, the commander of a great army, travel to a land where he knew no one, so he could be healed.

Naaman travelled to Israel with his servants, seven hundred and fifty pounds of silver, 6000 pieces of gold and ten changes of clothes as gifts. He took the letter from the king of Syria to the king of Israel.

In the letter, the king wrote, "Now this letter is to show that I am sending my servant Naaman to you. Cure his leprosy."

When the king of Israel read the letter, he tore his clothes to show he was sad and upset.

"Am I God? I do not have the power over life and death. So why did the king of Syria send a man sick with leprosy for me to heal? Think about it, and you will see that it is a trick. The king of Syria is trying to start a fight."

When Elisha, the man of God, heard that the king of Israel had torn his clothes, he sent a message to the king, "Why did you tear your clothes? Let Naaman come to me. Then he will know there is a prophet in Israel."

The king told Naaman what the prophet said, and Naaman went with his horses and chariots to Elisha's house and stood outside the door. Elisha sent a messenger to Naaman who said, "Go and wash in the Jordan River seven times. Then your skin will be healed, and you will be pure and clean."

Naaman became angry and left because he felt that the instruction the prophet gave him was too simple for someone of his status.
"I thought Elisha would at least come out and stand in front of me and call on the name of the Lord his God. I thought he would wave his hand over my body and heal the leprosy."

He was annoyed and turned to his servants, "Abanah and the Pharpar, the rivers of Damascus are better than all the waters in Israel. Why can't I wash in those rivers in Damascus and become clean?"

Still fuming with anger, he turned to leave. His servants went to him and encouraged him, "Father, if the prophet told you to do some great thing, you would do it, isn't that right? But he said, 'Wash, and you will be pure and clean.'"

After giving it some thought, Naaman did what the man of God said. He went down and dipped himself in the Jordan River seven times, and he became pure and clean. His skin became soft like the skin of a baby.
Naaman and all his servants went back to the man of God, filled with happiness. He stood before Elisha and said, "Look, I now know there is no God in all the earth except in Israel. Now please accept a gift from me."

Elisha refused the gift and said, "The Lord is the one I serve, and as surely as he lives, I will not accept any gift."

Naaman tried very hard to make Elisha take the gift, but he did not. This is because God's healing cannot be paid for. It is free — that is what makes it pure.

Then Naaman said, "If you will not accept this gift, at least do this for me. Let me have enough dirt from Israel to fill the baskets on two of my mules. I ask this because I will never again offer any burnt offering or sacrifice to any other gods. I will offer sacrifices only to the Lord! I pray that the Lord will forgive me for this: When my master, (the Syrian King) goes to the temple of Rimmon to worship that false god, he will want to lean on me for support. So I must bow down in the temple of Rimmon. I ask the Lord now to forgive me when that happens."

Then Elisha said to Naaman, "Go in peace."

The maidservant who advised Naaman to go to the prophet in Israel was an unnamed young girl who was kidnapped from her home to go serve a rich family in an entirely new and different land. She must have missed being with her loving family in Israel. However, regardless of her troubles, she was lovely and kind. In those times, people with leprosy were isolated from others. For her to be aware of her master's leprosy, she must have been close to her mistress. The girl had probably also said other things to her mistress in the past that were true because her mistress believed her and her master acted on her suggestion straightaway.

Further reading; 2 Kings 5:1-19.

☀️ Highlights

- The young servant girl feared God and had faith in God. She was a believer! She knew God for herself, not just what her parents and guardians taught her, and she knew what he could do for people who believed in Him. She was raised in a god-fearing home and she learned and observed for herself. She was a humble girl and knew her true identity in God.
Do you know your identity in God?

- She was a slave to the commander of the entire army of a powerful nation. However, this did not make her shy, timid, or stop her from giving a good suggestion. Imagine how confident and courageous she was to share her faith in God with her master, even when she was not asked for her opinion. However, she knew within her who God is and what He can do. If she did not speak up, her master would have suffered greatly because of leprosy.
It is so important to build your faith in God. When you have faith in God, you can come before his presence with boldness and confidence.

- The young servant girl had a kind and pure heart. After all, she was kidnapped from her family to serve in another country — the unfortunate circumstances and trauma gave her every reason to be unhappy and unkind. She truly loved God and this caused her to love and influence her master and mistress positively. When we love others fervently, it makes us see the best in them and overlook their limitations. Her master and mistress may have been kind towards her too.

- She did not only lead her master to where he would be healed but her master came to also experience the one and only true living God. I wonder how her healed master would have treated her after his return. As a part of God's kingdom, ask God to show you ways you can point your friends and family that are lost especially towards him.

- She had strong faith in God that kept her while she was living in a strange foreign land with foreign gods different from the faith and knowledge she was born into. Faith comes from hearing and hearing through the word of God.

- Even while away from her loving home, she still remembered all she learned and kept it within her and was ready to share with anyone around her. Despite the fact that she was kidnapped and brought to live with an idolatrous family, God kept her safe. No matter the environment you find yourself — whether in or outside your comfort zone — ensure you do not forget your godly values. Be unashamed to share God's goodness with others.

Ponder

- Do I know who I am in God and how God sees me?

- Am I too young to share my faith in God with others?

- In what different ways can I influence others positively around me, including those that do not share my faith in God (non-Christians)?

- Do I feel shy to do or say the right things? What makes me shy?

- In what ways can I be bolder as a believer in Christ?

- How do I behave when I find myself in unfortunate or unhappy situations?

Declare

- Lord help me to know you truly and deeply.

- Lord help me to live for you wherever I find myself.

- Lord help me to know I am your child and be conscious of your love wherever I find myself.

- Lord, fill my heart with your love and help me share it with others.

- I am strong and courageous and I influence everyone around me positively.

- May others experience God because of me.

MY NOTES

MY NOTES

ESTHER

King Ahasuerus, also known as Xerxes the Great, was the fifth king of Persia, and his throne sat in the capital city of Shushan. He reigned over one hundred and twenty-seven provinces, from India to Ethiopia.

In the third year of his reign, he made a feast for all his officials and servants — the powers of Persia and Media, the nobles, and the princes of the provinces were there too. The party lasted one hundred and eighty days and during this time he showed off the great wealth and splendour of his kingdom. After the one hundred and eighty days ended, King Xerxes held another feast for seven days in the courtyard of the palace garden. All the people who were in the citadel of Shushan, from the most important to the least important, were invited. The courtyard was decorated with white and blue linen curtains, held with cords of fine white and purple linen materials on silver rods and marble pillars. There were gold and silver couches on a mosaic pavement made of alabaster, white, black and turquoise marble. The king generously gave out plenty of wine which was served in golden cups. Every cup was different from the other.

Queen Vashti, the king's wife, made a feast for the women in the king's royal palace. On the seventh day of the feast, King Ahasuerus was in high spirits from drinking a lot of wine. He commanded his seven eunuchs; Mehuman, Biztha, Harbona, Bigtha, Abagtha, Zethar, and Carcas, to bring Queen Vashti to him, wearing her royal crown so he could show off her beauty to the people and officials. However, she refused to come before the king. The king was furious. He called for a meeting with his wise and highest men in the kingdom, according to the law; Shethar, Admatha, Tarshish, Meres, Marsena, and Memucan — who were also the seven princes of Persia and Media and had access to the king's presence.

He asked, "What shall we do to Queen Vashti? Because she didn't obey my command brought to her by the eunuchs?"

Memucan answered, "Queen Vashti has not only wronged the king, but also all the princes, and all the people who are in all the provinces of King Ahasuerus, because all the other women will hear about what Queen Vashti did, then they will stop obeying their husbands. Let the king give a royal command and let it be written in the laws of Persia and Medes that cannot be changed. The royal command should be that Vashti is never again to enter the presence of the King and let the king also give her royal position to someone else who is better than she is, so all women will respect their husbands both great and small."

The king was pleased with the advice he received and he sent letters to every province in the kingdom, written in different languages instructing every man to be a master in his home.

The king's servants who attended to him said, "Let beautiful young virgins be sought for the king and let the king appoint officers in all the provinces of his kingdom, to gather all the beautiful young virgins to the citadel of Shushan, into the women's quarters, under the custody of Hegai the king's eunuch in charge of the women. And let beauty preparations be given to them. The young maiden that pleases the king will become the queen instead of Vashti."

The king was happy with this plan.

There was a Jewish man named Mordecai, the son of Jair. He was a Benjamite living in Shushan. His great grandparents were carried away from Jerusalem as captives by Nebuchadnezzar, the king of Babylon. Mordecai had brought up Hadassah also called Esther, an orphan girl, who was his uncle's daughter. She had no father or mother, so he took her as his own daughter.

Esther was one of the young girls taken into the king's house in the care of Hegai the eunuch. She found favour with Hegai, so much so that he gave her extra beauty preparations and special food. Seven maidservants were given to tend to her and she was moved to the best location in the women's quarters. Every day, Mordecai walked in front of the courtyard of the women's quarters to check on Esther and to know how Esther fared. Nobody in the palace knew Esther was a Jew as Mordecai had asked her not to tell anyone.

The beauty preparations lasted twelve months; six months with myrrh oil and six months with perfumes and other ointments. After completing twelve months of beauty preparations, the young women were to take turns to go into the king's private harem. When it was Esther's turn, she did only what Hegai, the king's eunuch and custodian of the women, advised her to do. Esther had favour with everyone that saw her. In the tenth month, which is the month of Tebeth, and in the seventh year of King Ahasuerus' reign, Esther was taken into the king's royal palace. The king loved Esther more than all the other young women. She had grace and favour in his sight, so he set the royal crown upon her head and made her queen instead of Vashti. King Ahasuerus made a great feast — the Feast of Esther — for all his officials and servants. He proclaimed a holiday in the provinces and gave gifts generously to all. Even after she had been crowned and celebrated, no one in the palace knew that Esther was a Jew.

Mordecai was always by the king's palace because he was looking out for Esther. One day, while he sat at the king's gate, he uncovered the plan of two of the king's eunuchs, Bigthan and Teresh, who planned to harm the king. Mordecai told Queen Esther, and she informed the king. She also told the king that it was Mordecai who made the discovery of the treason. When the matter was investigated and found to be true, the treacherous eunuchs were both hanged on a tree before the king, just as it is written in the book of the Chronicles.

A short while after these occurrences, King Ahasuerus promoted Haman, the son of Hammedatha the Agagite, above the other princes. All the king's servants followed the king's commandment to bow to Haman. Only Mordecai refused to bow, not even when any of the king's servants told him off. When Haman was told that Mordecai was a Jew and refused to bow to him, he became annoyed and decided to destroy all the Jews throughout the whole kingdom of Ahasuerus.

In the twelfth year of King Ahasuerus' reign, Haman said to the king, "There are certain people scattered around in all the provinces of your kingdom. Their laws are different from all other people's, and they do not keep the king's laws. Therefore if it pleases the king, let a decree be written that they be destroyed. I will pay ten thousand talents of silver to those who do the work, to bring it into the king's treasuries."

The king responded to Haman, took off his signet ring, and gave it to Haman. He said, "The money and the people are given to you, to do with them as seems good to you."

Haman became the enemy of the Jews.

Haman commanded the king's scribes to write letters in different languages announcing that all Jews, whether young or old, be destroyed and killed, and their possessions be looted. The letters were sealed with the king's signet ring, making them decrees by the king, and sent by couriers into all the king's provinces on the thirteenth day of the twelfth month, which is the month of Adar. Haman was pleased and sat down to drink but the city of Shushan was distressed.
When Mordecai became aware of what was happening, he tore his clothes and put on sackcloth and ashes. He went out into the midst of the city and let out a loud and bitter cry. In every province where the king's decree was received, the Jews wept, wailed, fasted and many of them laid themselves in ashes and sackcloths. Mordecai could not enter the king's gate because he wore sackcloths.

Queen Esther's maids and eunuchs informed her that Mordecai was clothed in sackcloths and she became greatly distressed. She sent garments to clothe Mordecai and take his sackcloth away from him, but he did not accept them. Then Esther called Hathach, one of the king's eunuchs appointed to attend to her, and asked him to go to Mordecai, to know what his actions were about. Hathach met with Mordecai at the city square, before the king's gate, and Mordecai told him all that had happened. He told him the exact sum of the money that Haman had promised to pay to the king's treasuries to destroy the Jews and also he gave him the copy of the letter with the king's decree to show Queen Esther. Mordecai told Hathach to ask Esther to go to the king and plead for her people. Hathach relayed the message to the queen, and she sent him back to Mordecai with a message:

Esther 4:11 "All the king's servants, and the people of the king's provinces, do know, that whosoever, whether man or woman, shall come unto the king into the inner court, who is not called, there is one law for him, that he be put to death, except such to whom the king shall hold out the golden sceptre, that he may live: but I have not been called to come in unto the king these thirty days."

When Mordecai was told Esther's words, he replied:

Esther 4
13 "Do not think in your heart that you will escape in the king's palace any more than all the other Jews.
14 For if you remain completely silent at this time,

relief and deliverance will arise for the Jews from another place, but you and your father's house will perish. Yet who knows whether you have come to the kingdom for such a time as this?"

15 Then Esther told them to reply to Mordecai:

16 "Go, gather all the Jews who are present in Shushan, and fast for me; neither eat nor drink for three days, night or day. My maids and I will fast likewise. And so I will go to the king, which is against the law; and if I perish, I perish!"

17 So Mordecai went his way and did according to all that Esther commanded him.

On the third day, Queen Esther wore her royal robes and stood at the inner court of the king's palace while the king sat on his throne. When King Ahasuerus saw Esther, she found favour with him. He held out his golden sceptre towards her and she touched the top of the sceptre.

He asked her, "What's your wish, Queen Esther? And I would give you up to half the kingdom."

She answered, " If the King is pleased, I am inviting you, the king and Haman for a banquet I have prepared for you".

The King was delighted and called Haman to be at the

queen's banquet. At the banquet of wine, the king asked Esther again, "What is your request and I will give you, up to half of the kingdom."

Esther replied, "If the king is pleased, I am inviting you, the king, and Haman to another banquet I have prepared for you."

Haman made his way home joyful, ready to tell his friends and wife, Zeresh, how the queen had prepared a special banquet for him and the king. On his way out, he saw Mordecai seated at the king's gate.

Haman's hatred for Mordecai was so much that he could not stand the sight of him at the king's gate. That very day, he instructed that gallows be made, so he could use them to hang Mordecai to death.

That night, the king could not sleep. He commanded the servants to bring and read the book of records of the chronicles and memorable deeds to him. He found out that Mordecai had not been honoured for saving his life after he exposed the plot of the two eunuchs to harm him.

The next day, the king called Haman and asked him, "What should be done for a man the king delights to honour?"

Haman thought it was him the king had in mind, so he

told the king, "Let the man wear the king's robe, a royal crown and ride on the horseback in the city square."

When Haman found out that it was Mordecai the king intended to honour, and Mordecai was treated with prestige, he became even more angry and bitter.

Queen Esther soon celebrated the second banquet with the king and Haman. During the banquet of wine, the king asked Esther again, "What is your request and I will give you, up to half of the kingdom."

Esther replied, " If I have found favour with you and if you are pleased with me, oh King, I ask that my life and that of my people be given back because we have been sold by an enemy to be killed and destroyed."

It was at this moment the king realised that his queen was a Jew. When the king found out Haman was the enemy of the Jews, he was upset and instructed one of his eunuchs, Harbonah, to hang Haman on the very gallows that he had prepared for Mordecai.

The king took the signet ring from Haman and gave it to Mordecai and he was appointed in place of Haman. Queen Esther pleaded with the king to have Haman's plot to destroy the Jews in all the king's provinces reversed and put his new decree into writing. King Ahasuerus approved and urged Queen Esther and

Mordecai to write a letter regarding the Jews as they pleased and seal it with the signet ring. Mordecai wrote the decree of the king in a document and sent it to every province quickly by courier on royal horses.

The Jews all over the province of Shushan rejoiced and made a feast to celebrate. Many people in the land became Jews because they became afraid of the Jews. On that day, the people that hated the Jews were all overpowered by them. The Jews destroyed the enemies that hated them with swords, including Haman's ten sons.
All the princes of the provinces, the satraps, the governors, and all the king's workers, helped the Jews because they feared Mordecai. Mordecai was great in the king's house, and his fame spread throughout all the provinces. He became greater and greater as time went on. All the Jews gathered together to celebrate their victory over their enemies. It was a day of feasting, rejoicing, resting and exchanging presents with each other. This celebration was done on the fourteenth day of the month of Adar and they called it the "The Feast of Purim".

Queen Esther and Mordecai made the festival official. He wrote all the commands down as a book of remembrance for the people and their descendants. He sent out letters to the Jews telling them to celebrate this feast yearly according to the instructions in every province and town. It was a day the Jews rested from their enemies and their mourning was turned into joy. The Jews still celebrate the Purim festival.

Further reading; Esther 1 - 10.

💡 Highlights

A FAST - Esther fasted for three days to seek God's help in prayer, so that her people, the Jews, would not be killed.

Taking a fast is voluntary, for a long or short period of time, to quieten yourself and spend time with God. You can fast from food, TV, social media, shopping, a favourite treat or a hobby — this is not an exhaustive list. Fast so you can spend a period of time with God and learn more about him. During your fast, read your bible, worship, listen to a Christian podcast or watch a sermon and meditate in God's presence.

OBEDIENCE - It was not always convenient for Esther but she obeyed her cousin, Mordecai's instructions not to reveal her identity as a Jew initially. And subsequently, to go before the king so she could save her people. She had a reward for her obedience. She stepped out of her comfort zone as a queen and delivered her nation.

For you to grow as a believer in Christ, you have to learn to trust God and obey him. If you love God, you will obey his commands. Be consistent in the little things and you will grow into bigger things.

HUMILITY - Esther was so humble that she did not think to herself, "After all, I am so beautiful, what more can the king's eunuch Hegai teach me?" She understood that having different beauty regimens and showing up for events was not enough to make her a queen — she needed a good character to lead others.

You should have a teachable spirit and be ready to learn and improve upon yourself with every opportunity. Feedback is valuable and when you receive one use it wisely. Do not always be defensive when you are taught.

FAVOUR - God's favour was upon Esther. She was beautiful and she also had a good character. She found favour before people because of these attributes. Everyone that saw her loved her. Although there was an unpleasant and difficult situation, the king granted Esther all her desires.
You should not have one or the other. Being handsome or beautiful with a good character is desirable.

WISDOM - Esther was wise. She did not approach the king without a strategy. She first of all fasted and asked God what to do before she prepared herself, wore her royal robes and had a banquet fit for the king. Remember she learned well and followed the instructions of Hegai, the eunuch, during her training period. She was well prepared for all the challenges she was going to experience.

You are not too young to be wise. All your past experiences help you to make better decisions today and in the future. When next you face a challenge, pause and say a prayer, asking God to show you a way out of the challenge. Then be attentive to God's direction. Remember, when God leads and directs us, there is no confusion but peace.

FEARLESS - Esther and Mordecai were courageous. They were ready to risk their lives to save their people by coming before the king. They did not let fear stop them from taking action. Esther was chosen in that season to deliver her people.
What are the bold steps you need to take in becoming who God has made you to be? It may be today or in the future, but at different times in your life, you will have to make bold decisions. Trust God to help you and take the first step. Do it afraid!

MINDSET - Esther did not see herself as an orphan or a slave-girl but as a deliverer God could use to deliver his people. She went from an orphan and slave girl to becoming a queen that God will use for His agenda. Do not look down on yourself. You are not inferior. Your past circumstances do not predict your future. See yourself through God's eyes. Start by reading a verse of scripture a day to know what God thinks and says about you.

Ponder

- How do you see yourself?

- Are you fearful? If you are, what makes you afraid?

- Are you aware that true wisdom comes from God? God said we should ask him for wisdom and he would give us generously.

Declare

- Lord fill me with your wisdom, knowledge and understanding.

- I work by faith in God and not by the current situation.

- I have favour with God and others.

- I have the mind of Christ.

MY NOTES

MY NOTES

JEREMIAH

Jeremiah was the son of Hilkiah, and was born into a family of priests. He lived in the town of Anathoth, a town that belonged to the tribe of Benjamin.

He started his service to God as a teenage boy. In the thirteenth year of Josiah's reign as the king of Judah, God started speaking to Jeremiah and God chose the young prophet to be his spokesman to the people of Judah. God continued to speak to Jeremiah during the reign of Jehoiakim, the son of Josiah, as king of Judah and during the eleven years and five months that Zedekiah, another son of Josiah reigned as the king of Judah. In the fifth month of Zedekiah's reign, the people who lived in Jerusalem were taken away into exile in Babylon.

God Calls Jeremiah;

Jeremiah 1
4 The Lord's message came to me:

5 "Before I made you in your mother's womb,
    I knew you.
Before you were born,
    I chose you for a special work.
    I chose you to be a prophet to the nations."
6 Then I said, "But, Lord God, I do not know how to speak. I am only a boy."
7 But the Lord said to me,
"Don't say, 'I am only a boy.'
    You must go everywhere I send you
    and say everything I tell you to say.
8 Don't be afraid of anyone.
    I am with you, and I will protect you."
This message is from the Lord.
9 Then the Lord reached out with his hand and touched my mouth. He said to me,
"Jeremiah, I am putting my words in your mouth.
10 Today I have put you in charge of nations and kingdoms.
    You will pull up and tear down.
You will destroy and overthrow.
    You will build up and plant."

Jeremiah lived in very challenging times. He was ignored, rejected and persecuted by the people God sent him to preach to, nevertheless, he served God faithfully for about forty years. God sent him to tell the leaders and the people to repent from their wicked ways and from practising idolatry but they did not listen. They mocked him. Jeremiah warned the leaders and people, that if they persisted with their sinful living, God's judgement would come upon them and they would be responsible for their destruction.

The people refused to listen to God's messages and not long after, God allowed Babylon to put the people in captivity.

Jeremiah was sometimes called the 'Weeping Prophet'. He was passionate and had a tender heart towards the leaders and people of Judah, yet, they ignored and mocked him. His family members also turned against him. Jeremiah never had a wife or children and he was alone. Regardless of his hardships, he remained faithful to God.

Jeremiah wrote the book of Lamentations, which is found in the old testament in the bible. He told tales of how and when Jerusalem was destroyed and the people were held captive in Babylon.

Jeremiah is also known for foretelling the coming of the Messiah.

Further reading; Jeremiah 1, 2, 9, 12.

☀ Highlights

CHOSEN - Jeremiah was called and chosen from his mother's womb, before he was born, to be a prophet to the nations.
God chose you. You did not bring yourself into the world. He has a reason and purpose for you on earth so do not look down on yourself because he called you to make a difference for him on earth. So look to God and ask Him to reveal to you, the plans He has for your life

SUCCESS - Jeremiah may not have seemed successful to everyone because he had no material possessions but he was a success to God. He was one of the major prophets in the bible. He obeyed and served God faithfully. He proclaimed God's word courageously, regardless of whether the people listened to him or not.

God rates success because he is our maker and knows why he created us. To be successful (God's standard) in life, you need to seek God with all your heart, ask him what his plans for your life are and earnestly follow it. As you relate with God, you have to trust and obey every instruction he gives you. Remember, every person has a different call in life so you need to stay true to yours and do not compare.

OBEDIENT - Jeremiah did all God told Jeremiah to do. Although he was young and lived in challenging times, he served and obeyed God faithfully, even when it was

not convenient. It was God's will first, before his own will.
If you love God, you will obey him. Ask him to help you obey him especially when it may seem difficult.

TREND - All Jeremiah wanted to do was please God, his maker, and this made him unpopular and disesteemed amongst the people. He was thoroughly despised, but he never let go of his ambition to please God.

Because you love God so much, your earnest goal in life should be to please him and make him happy with the way you live your life. Let it be evident in what you say and in your actions that you are a child of God. It's okay not to trend and be popular. What matters most is to live a life that honours God. You are God's beloved regardless, so it is irrelevant to him whether or not you trend at school or on social media.

QUALIFICATION - Jeremiah felt unqualified. He reminded God that he was just a boy. However, he forgot that God made him and clearly knew he was young, but he still chose him to do his work. You may be looking down on yourself but God does not. He sees you as his special one — the one he created for a special purpose. God has given you natural gifts and talents and he wants you to use them all for his glory. Your life cannot be determined by those who like or dislike you, what you have or do not have, whether you are male or female, or how you look. You are made in God's image and likeness and that is more than enough.

Ponder

- Am I too young to answer God's call?

- Who is a Prophet?

- How do I feel about popularity?

Declare

- Lord increase my faith and help me trust and obey you at all times.

- I am complete in Christ Jesus and he is head over all.

- I can do all things through Christ who gives me strength.

MY NOTES

MY NOTES

DANIEL

During the third year of King Jehoiakim's reign as the king of Judah, Jerusalem was attacked by Nebuchadnezzar, the king of Babylon. God allowed Nebuchadnezzar to capture king Jehoiakim and other nobles and royals. He also took items from God's temple and he kept them in his own temple. King Nebuchadnezzar instructed Ashpenaz, the highest officer in charge of the palace, to choose some boys captured from Israel, including the royals from Judah, and train them to serve in the palace. These chosen boys were to be healthy, wise, handsome, smart and quick to learn so they could be able to serve in the king's palace. Ashpenaz was to teach them the language and writings of the Chaldeans and the boys were to be trained for three years before they could serve the king. The boys were also expected to eat and drink from the king's table.

The young captives from Judah chosen were Daniel,

Mishael, Hananiah and Azariah. Ashpenaz changed their names — to Daniel, he gave the name Belteshazzar, to Hananiah, he gave the name Shadrach, to Mishael, he gave the name Meshach, and to Azariah, he gave the name Abed-Nego.

Daniel was a teenager when he was taken into captivity in Babylon. He made up his mind not to eat any of the delicacies from the king's table because they would make him unclean. He asked Ashpenaz for permission for him and his friends not to eat from the king's table. Ashpenaz told Daniel in response that all the young boys were supposed to eat from the king's table and the king could kill him, Ashpenaz, if Daniel looked worse than the other boys in training. However, God made the chief officer show compassion and kindness to Daniel. Daniel asked Ashpenaz to give him and his friends vegetables and water and after ten days, compare how they looked with the other boys. The Chief officer agreed and put a guard in charge of Daniel and his three friends.

After ten days, Daniel and his friends looked healthier than the other boys that ate delicacies and drank from the king's table. So the guard gave them only vegetables and water.
God filled these four boys with wisdom, knowledge, and an understanding of different kinds of writings and science. Daniel especially had understanding in all dreams and visions.

After three years, Ashpenaz brought all the young boys he trained before Nebuchadnezzar. The king talked with all of them and found none of them to be better than Daniel, Shadrach, Mishael and Abednego, so he chose them to serve in the palace. They were ten times better than all the magicians and wise men in the palace. Daniel served the king until the first year of King Cyrus' reign as the king of Babylon.

In Nebuchadnezzar's second year as king, he had a dream that troubled his mind and he could not sleep. He called all the magicians, astrologers, sorcerers and wise men to tell him what his dream meant and to interpret it. They all tried but none of them could do so. The king promised to reward and honour whoever could interpret his dream, but if they could not, he would give orders to have them chopped into pieces and their houses destroyed.

"What you are asking for is impossible," the king's wise men said to the king, "No one on earth can do what the king is asking. Not even the greatest and wisest king has ever asked his wise men to do such a thing."

When king Nebuchadnezzar heard this, he was very angry and he ordered that all the wise men of Babylon be killed. The king's men were also sent to look for Daniel and his friends and put them all to death.
Daniel politely asked Arioch, the commander of the

King's guard, why the king gave such cruel orders. Arioch explained what happened. When Daniel heard the whole story, he went before the king and asked for some more time to interpret the dream for him. Daniel went home and told his friends Shadrach, Meshach and Abednego what had been going on. He asked them to pray to God Almighty and plead for his help and mercy concerning the mystery so they and the wise men of Babylon would not be killed.

During the night, the mystery of the king's dream was explained to Daniel in a vision. So Daniel praised God Almighty.

Daniel 2

20 He said,

"Praise God's name forever and ever!

   Power and wisdom belong to him.

21 He changes the times and seasons.

   He gives power to kings,

   and he takes their power away.

He gives wisdom to people, so they become wise.

   He lets people learn things and become wise.

22 He knows hidden secrets that are hard to understand.

   Light lives with him,

   so he knows what is in the dark and secret places.

23 God of my ancestors, I thank you and praise you.

You gave me wisdom and power.
You told us what we asked for.
You told us about the king's dream."

Daniel went to Arioch and asked that he be taken to the King to interpret his dream. King Nebuchadnezzar asked Daniel if he was truly able to tell him what he saw in his dream and interpret it.

Daniel 2

27 Daniel answered, "King Nebuchadnezzar, no wise man, no man who does magic, and no Chaldean could tell the king the secret things he has asked about.

28 But there is a God in heaven who tells secret things. God has given King Nebuchadnezzar dreams to show him what will happen later. This was your dream, and this is what you saw while lying on your bed:

29 King, as you were lying there on your bed, you began thinking about what might happen in the future. God can tell people about secret things—he has shown you what will happen in the future.

30 God also told this secret to me, not because I have greater wisdom than other men, but so that you, king, may know what it means. In that way, you will understand what went through your mind.

31 "King, in your dream you saw a large statue in front of you that was very large and shiny. It was very impressive.

32 The head of the statue was made from pure gold. Its chest and the arms were made from silver. The belly and upper part of the legs were made from bronze.

33 The lower part of the legs was made from iron. Its feet were made partly of iron and partly of clay.

34 While you were looking at the statue, you saw a rock that was cut loose, but not by human hands. Then the rock hit the statue on its feet of iron and clay and smashed them.

35 Then the iron, the clay, the bronze, the silver, and the gold broke to pieces all at the same time. And all the pieces became like chaff on a threshing floor in the summertime. The wind blew them away, and there was nothing left. No one could tell that a statue had ever been there. Then the rock that hit the statue became a very large mountain and filled up the whole earth.

36 "That was your dream. Now we will tell the king what it means.

37 King, you are the most important king. The God of heaven has given you a kingdom, power, strength, and

glory.

38 He has given you control, and you rule over people and the wild animals and the birds. Wherever they live, God has made you ruler over them all. King Nebuchadnezzar, you are that head of gold on the statue.

39 "Another kingdom will come after you, but it will not be as great as your kingdom. Next, a third kingdom will rule over the earth—that is the bronze part.

40 Then there will be a fourth kingdom. That kingdom will be strong like iron. Just as iron breaks things and smashes them to pieces, that fourth kingdom will break all the other kingdoms and smash them to pieces.

41 "You saw that the feet and toes of the statue were partly clay and partly iron. That means the fourth kingdom will be a divided kingdom. It will have some of the strength of iron in it just as you saw the iron mixed with clay.

42 The toes of the statue were partly iron and partly clay. So the fourth kingdom will be partly strong like iron and partly weak like clay.

43 You saw the iron mixed with clay, but iron and clay don't completely mix together. In the same way the

people of the fourth kingdom will be a mixture. They will not be united as one people.

44 "During the time of the kings of the fourth kingdom, the God of heaven will set up another kingdom that will continue forever. It will never be destroyed. And it will be the kind of kingdom that cannot be passed on to another group of people. This kingdom will crush all the other kingdoms. It will bring them to an end, but that kingdom itself will continue forever.

45 "King Nebuchadnezzar, you saw a rock cut from a mountain, but no one cut that rock. The rock broke the iron, the bronze, the clay, the silver, and the gold to pieces. In this way God showed you what will happen in the future. The dream is true, and you can trust that this is what it means."

When Daniel had finished telling the king his dream and its interpretation, Nebuchadnezzar bowed with his face down before Daniel to honour him.

Daniel 2

47 Then the king said to Daniel, "I know for sure your God is the God over all gods and the Lord over all kings. He tells people about things they cannot know. I know this is true because you were able to tell these secret things to me."

King Nebuchadnezzar gave Daniel lots of gifts and promoted Daniel to be the Governor of the Babylon Province. He also put him in charge of the other wise men.
Daniel asked the king to promote his three friends and he did. Shadrach, Meshach and Abednego were made Administrators over the province of Babylon.

Sometime later, King Nebuchadnezzar had a gold idol made. It was sixty cubits high and six cubits wide. He set the idol on the plain of Dura, in the province of Babylon. The king called the satraps, administrators, governors, counsellors, treasurers, judges, rulers and all the other officials in his province to come to the dedication ceremony for the gold idol. All these men came together and stood in front of the idol.

An official made an announcement in a loud voice, "All you people from many nations and language groups, listen to me. This is what you are all commanded to do: As soon as you hear the sound of horns, flutes, lyres, sambucas, harps, bagpipes, and all the other musical instruments, you must bow down to worship King Nebuchadnezzar's gold idol. Whoever does not bow down to worship this gold idol will be thrown into a very hot furnace immediately."

As soon as they heard the sound of all the musical instruments, all the peoples of different language groups and nations bowed down and worshipped the gold idol except Shadrach, Meshach and Abednego. They ignored the king's orders to worship his gold idol. Some of the Chaldeans reported this to the king and Nebuchadnezzar was very angry with them.

Daniel 3

16 Shadrach, Meshach, and Abednego answered the king, "Nebuchadnezzar, we don't need to explain these things to you.

17 If you throw us into the hot furnace, the God we serve can save us. And if he wants to, he can save us from your power.

18 But even if God does not save us, we want you to know, King, that we refuse to serve your gods. We will not worship the gold idol you have set up."

King Nebuchadnezzar was furious with Daniel's friends and he gave an order for the furnace to be made seven times hotter than it usually was. He commanded some of the strongest soldiers in his army to throw them into the hot furnace. Shadrach, Meshach and Abednego were tied up and thrown into the furnace wearing their robes, turbans, trousers and other clothing. The furnace was so hot that the flames of the fire killed the soldiers who threw them in.

Daniel 3

24 Then King Nebuchadnezzar jumped to his feet. He

was very surprised and he asked his advisors, "We tied only three men, and we threw only three men into the fire. Is that right?"

His advisors said, "Yes, King."

25 The king said, "Look! I see four men walking around in the fire. They are not tied up and they are not burned. The fourth man looks like an angel."

26 Then Nebuchadnezzar went to the opening of the hot furnace. He shouted, "Shadrach, Meshach, and Abednego, come out! Servants of the Most High God, come here!"

So Shadrach, Meshach, and Abednego came out of the fire.

27 When they came out, the satraps, prefects, governors, and royal advisors crowded around them. They could see that the fire had not burned Shadrach, Meshach, and Abednego. Their bodies were not burned at all. Their hair was not burned, and their robes were not burned. They didn't even smell as if they had been near fire.

28 Then Nebuchadnezzar said, "Praise the God of Shadrach, Meshach, and Abednego. Their God has sent his angel and saved his servants from the fire!

These three men trusted their God and refused to obey my command. They were willing to die instead of serving or worshiping any other god.

29 So I now make this law: Anyone from any nation or language group who says anything against the God of Shadrach, Meshach, and Abednego will be cut into pieces, and their house will be destroyed until it is a pile of dirt and ashes. No other god can save his people like this."

30 Then the king gave Shadrach, Meshach, and Abednego more important jobs in the province of Babylon.

Amongst the dreams and visions recorded in the book of Daniel was King Nebuchadnezzar's second dream of the "big strong tree", which Daniel also interpreted. After King Nebuchadnezzar's reign, Daniel served under three more kings — Belshazzar, the son of Nebuchadnezzar, Darius the Medes and Cyrus the Persian. He was the one who explained the meaning of the 'handwriting on the wall' to King Belshazzar. As a Prophet and a Governor, Daniel lived in exile in Babylon for seventy years.

During the reign of King Darius, Daniel was made one of the three Governors in Babylon who were put in control of one hundred and twenty Satraps to ensure the kingdom was working properly.

Daniel was an exceptional Governor with good character and great ability. This made the king plan to make him govern over the whole kingdom. When the other Governors heard this, they were jealous and tried to find reasons to accuse Daniel falsely but they found nothing because he was an honest and faithful man. They knew they could not find any faults unless it was something to do with the law of his God. So the other two Governors and all the Satraps went to King Darius as a group and asked the king to make a law that everyone must obey.

"Give orders that for the next thirty days, any person who prays to any god or man except to you, Your Majesty, will be thrown into the den of lions," they said to the king.

The king agreed, made the law and signed it.

Daniel usually prayed three times a day and even though he heard this new law, he still went home to pray to God, his heavenly father, giving thanks and asking him for help. His window was open and faced the direction of Jerusalem. When the group of men saw Daniel praying, they reported to the king and reminded him of the law he had signed, which could not be changed or cancelled. When King Darius realised Daniel had to be thrown into the lions' den, he was overwhelmed with sadness.

Daniel 6:16 So King Darius gave the order. They brought Daniel and threw him into the lions' den. The king said to Daniel, "May the God you serve save you!"

God did save Daniel because he was innocent! He sent his angel to save Daniel by shutting the mouths of the lions so they could not hurt him.

That night Darius could not sleep. He ate nothing and had no entertainment because he was anxious about Daniel. Early the next morning he ran to the lion's den.

Daniel 6
20 He was very worried. When he got to the lions' den, he called to Daniel. He said, "Daniel, servant of the living God, has your God been able to save you from the lions? You always serve your God."
21 Daniel answered, "King, live forever!
22 My God sent his angel to save me. The angel closed the lions' mouths. The lions have not hurt me because my God knows I am innocent. I never did anything wrong to you, King."

Darius was so happy that Daniel was alive and he gave orders to have him brought out of the den. When he came out, he had no wounds on his body. The king commanded that the group of men that accused Daniel and their families be thrown into the den instead. The lions ate them up even before they got to the bottom of the den.

Daniel 6

25 Then King Darius wrote this letter to all the people from other nations and language groups all around the world:

Greetings:

26 I am making a new law. This law is for people in every part of my kingdom. All of you must fear and respect the God of Daniel.

Daniel's God is the living God;
  he lives forever.
His kingdom will never be destroyed.
  His rule will never end.
27 God helps and saves people.
  He does amazing miracles in heaven and on earth.
He saved Daniel from the lions.
28 So Daniel was successful during the time Darius was king and when Cyrus the Persian was king.

Further reading; Daniel 1 - 12.

Highlights

DEVOUT - Daniel prayed regularly and studied the word of God. His relationship with God was so deep that even when he was faced with trouble, he prayed and trusted God for help. God answered his prayers because he is a faithful father.

God wants a relationship with you too. When you draw near to God he draws near to you. You start to know God for yourself and grow in him too. God does not need you to be perfect first; he wants you to come to him as you are and in him, you will find perfection. Anyone who comes to God must believe that God exists and he rewards everyone that seeks him.

Have you wondered how to pray or what to pray about? Jesus taught us 'The Lord's Prayer'. Please pray and learn below.

"THE LORD's PRAYER"

Our Father in heaven,
Hallowed be Your name.
Your kingdom come.
Your will be done on earth as it is in heaven.
Give us this day our daily bread.
And forgive us our debts, as we forgive our debtors.
And do not lead us into temptation, but deliver us from

the evil one.
For Yours is the kingdom and the power and the glory forever.
Amen.

Here are different types of prayers but you can start with the simpler prayers and build yourself towards the other types of prayers.

Remember, when praying, you should always go to God in faith. A simple approach to prayer is the A.C.T.S model.

A - Adoration (Praise and worship God)
C - Confession (Admit and repent of any sin or wrongdoing)
T - Thanksgiving (Express gratitude to God, giving Him thanks for everything)
S - Supplication (Appeal and ask God for your needs and for the needs of others).

Matthew 6
5 "When you pray, don't be like the hypocrites. They love to stand in the synagogues and on the street corners and pray loudly. They want people to see them. The truth is, that's all the reward they will get.
6 But when you pray, you should go into your room and close the door. Then pray to your Father. He is there in

that private place. He can see what is done in private, and he will reward you.

7 "And when you pray, don't be like the people who don't know God. They say the same things again and again. They think that if they say it enough, their god will hear them.

8 Don't be like them. Your Father knows what you need before you ask him.

WISDOM - Daniel and his friends were found to be ten times wiser than all the magicians and enchanters that were in the kingdom. While in captivity, Daniel was given a different name — Belshazzar — but it did not matter to him. Yes, our names are important and significant, but because he was in captivity, he was limited. He had to choose his battles. He was wise enough to know what mattered. For instance, it was more important to him that he ate healthily and did not defile his body with food served to Babylonian idols. Scripture tells us that our bodies are the temple of the Holy Spirit.

Daniel was raised by godly parents or guardians and he developed a personal relationship with God. He had good character, was intelligent and good looking. Remember, it is God who gives the features that humans call beautiful or handsome. It is God who gives us the wisdom and knowledge that make other people call us clever or intelligent. So be mindful not to be prideful when you get accolades. Do not get carried away with your looks and knowledge. Use them for God's glory — it would give Him great pleasure.

FRIENDSHIPS - Although Daniel was a captive in Babylon — a land of idolatry — he surrounded himself with godly friends — Shadrach, Meshach and Abednego. When Daniel was promoted, he made sure his three close friends were promoted too.

As you rise in life, raise your close friends along with you, and remember to pray for your friends too. It is not an opportunity to boast and compete with each other. Imagine how lonely it would have been for him without them. He needed his friends like we all do to have a good time, lean on, get advice and support each other. There is no way to enjoy life without good friends, but you must choose them wisely. You cannot be the only good one in the bunch because bad company corrupts good manners. Remember as God raises you, bring your good friends along too.

BOLD & COURAGEOUS - Daniel's friends; Shadrach, Meshach and Abednego were courageous when they refused to bow to King Nebuchadnezzar's gold idol, even though their lives were at risk. They had more respect for God than the king so they obeyed God instead.

We are to worship and serve God only, not idols. An idol is not only a physical image or statue. It can be anything or anyone you greatly admire or love more than God.

Daniel was courageous when he asked for vegetables and water — a choice different from the palace norms. He chose to pray even when King Darius decree said otherwise and he was at risk of dying in the lion's den.
When you find yourself under pressure from your friends or in situations that would compromise you and your faith in God, don't bow to such things. Simply trust God with your whole heart and he will deliver you.

FAITHFUL - Daniel, Shadrach, Meshach and Abednego were loyal to God even though they could have made excuses not to serve God. After all, they were slaves and were surrounded by idolatrous people. They also had to obey the king. However, they obeyed God even when it was not convenient and were at risk of losing their lives. They could have eaten or drank as they wanted for comfort because they were held in exile. Yet, they did not compromise their faith regardless of the pressure from authority.
At different times in your life you may come under pressure from friends, studies or work and your faith in God will be tested, but don't give in; hold fast to your faith in God nevertheless. God is faithful and you can

trust Him. He will not let you be tempted beyond what you can bear — and even when you are tempted, he will provide a way out so that you can endure such temptations.

GIFTED - Daniel, Shadrach, Meschach and Abednego were gifted boys and they acquired skills when they had three years of palace training with Asphenaz. The King could not help but promote them to become officials in his kingdom because they stood out and were excellent amongst the other boys that trained alongside.

One of the different ways God speaks to us is through dreams and visions and there are many examples of this recorded in the bible. The king's dream and some of Daniel's dreams were instructions of things that would happen. With God's help, Daniel was able to interpret the king's dreams and his dreams as well. God would not have given a dream or shown symbols that could not be interpreted, so he used Daniel to explain these mysteries for his glory.

If you have dreams of the night, remember Daniel prayed and asked God for the wisdom and understanding needed to interpret dreams. He wrote his dream down and worked with its summary. One time, when he could not understand his dream, Angel Gabriel helped him. Remember how great God is — he is the maker of the entire universe and he cares about you, no matter how young you are. Yes, you are so important to Him!

God says ask and you will receive, seek and you will find. You can ask about your dreams too. The explanation of your dreams and their interpretation comes from God and not from a psychic or the internet.

SUCCESSFUL - Daniel was a Governor in the province of Babylon. He served four kings successfully. Daniel became a success because God was with him. He, in turn, used his influence to bring God glory. His relationship with God, while in training and even after, was the centre of his life. Daniel led as a Governor based on godly values.

God expects you to be excellent in all you do — whether it is in your studies, sports, craft, or as a leader. Let every aspect of your life be based on godly values. Step out of your comfort zone and use your God-given gifts to serve others and watch how God will help you succeed for his glory. Look for different ways to improve, so you can become the best version of yourself.

Whatever you do, do it well!

Ponder

- Do I truly have faith in God?

- Do I have the courage to live for Christ and stand out for Him anywhere?

- What does prayer mean to me? How often do I pray?

- Even when no one is watching me, am I still faithful to God?

Declare

- I love your word oh Lord, I read and hear your word. My faith increases!

- I am born of God, I belong to God, I am an overcomer, I've overcome the world and I walk daily in victory. He that is in me is greater than he that is in the world.

MY NOTES

MY NOTES

THE BOY WITH BREAD AND FISHES

Jesus and his disciples were amongst a huge crowd of people. They had just returned from their mission work and the disciples shared all they did and how they taught the people in the places Jesus had sent them to. Because of the huge number of people, Jesus and his disciples did not have time to eat.

"Come with me. We will go to a quiet place to be alone. There we can get some rest," Jesus said to the disciples.

They went away in a boat, and they were on the Sea of Galilee, also known as the Sea of Tiberias, to go to a deserted place, where no one lived. A great crowd of people saw them and followed Jesus by foot because they saw many miraculous signs and how Jesus had been healing the sick.

Jesus went up the mountain and sat there with his disciples. It was almost time for the Jewish Passover festival.

Jesus soon looked up and he saw a crowd of people coming towards Him. He had compassion on them and received them warmly. He taught them about the kingdom of God and healed the sick people in the crowd.

Jesus' disciples came to Him and said, "This is a deserted place, it is already getting late. Send the crowd away so they can go to the nearby villages and buy themselves some food."

Jesus refused!

"Where can we buy enough bread for all these people to eat?" Jesus asked his disciple, Philip.

This question was asked to test Philip. Jesus already knew what he planned to do.

Philip answered Jesus, "We would all have to work a month to buy enough bread for each person here to have only a little piece!"

Andrew, the brother of Simon Peter, another disciple of Jesus spoke, "There is a boy with five loaves of barley bread and two little fish. But that is not enough for so many people."

"Tell everyone to sit down," Jesus replied.

The place was filled with grass, and there were about 5000 men present. There were also many women and children there that day. Everyone in the crowd sat in groups. Jesus then took the five barley loaves of bread and two fishes, looked up to heaven, blessed it, broke it, and gave the food to his disciples to share to the crowd. He gave the people as much as they wanted. They all had plenty to eat and were filled.
When they finished, Jesus said to his disciples, "Gather the pieces of fish and bread that were not eaten. Don't waste anything."

The people had started eating with only five loaves of barley bread, but by the time the disciples gathered the pieces that were left, there were twelve baskets filled with the pieces of food that were leftover.

The crowd saw this miracle that Jesus did and said amongst themselves, "He must be the Prophet whose coming was spoken of in times past by many Prophets. "

Jesus knew that the people planned to come get him and make him their king. So he left and went into the hills alone.

Further reading; Matthew 14:13-21, John 6:1-15, Mark 6:30-44, Luke 9:10-17.

Highlights

- You can come to Jesus anytime, any day. He won't turn his back on you. He is loving and compassionate and never too busy to respond to our needs. Jesus has feelings too! When you are suffering, remember Jesus is hurting with you and he is compassionate to heal you.

- Jesus is so loving that he cares for not only your spiritual food and nourishment but also for your physical nourishment. Jesus knew the people were hungry. He fed them with the word of God and also fed their stomachs with food.

- I wonder if the young boy was the only one in the large crowd with some food. Or was he simply kindhearted and willing to share his food with people he did not know? This unnamed boy will always be remembered for his generosity and for having a small packed lunch of bread and fish that Jesus miraculously multiplied. Whatever we give Jesus, no matter how little — whether it is your gift, talent, treasure, or time, he can multiply it for his glory.

- Jesus looked to heaven because the power to do miracles, signs and wonders come only from God Almighty. He is the only true source of power. When situations look impossible, it can be an opportunity for a miracle to happen if you trust God. Jesus did the miracle to show he can multiply the little you give him. We also learn that Jesus does not like us being wasteful, not just with food, but with our time and talents.

The crowd and Jesus' disciples were all astonished by this great miracle and their faith in God grew.

Ponder

- Do I believe in miracles? Who is the source of miracles?

- When I am sick, or others are sick, do I remember to pray, asking Jesus for healing?

- What are my needs? Do you trust God to provide for you?

- Am I too young to be generous/ to share my gifts with others?

- What do I have Jesus can use?

Declare

- God is my source and I lack nothing.

- I believe in miracles and that Jesus heals.

- Lord, help me to be kind and generous.

- Lord, use anything I have to bless others.

- I am not lost in the crowd. I stand out for Jesus.

MY NOTES

MY NOTES

RHODA THE SERVANT GIRL

King Herod wanted to harm believers in Christ, so he arrested some members of the church. He ordered James, the brother of John, to be killed with a sword. This made many of the Jews happy, so he decided to also arrest Peter during the Festival of Unleavened Bread. Peter was put in jail and was guarded by sixteen soldiers. Herod planned to bring Peter before the people to be tried, but he thought to wait until after the Passover festival. While Peter was kept in jail, the church was constantly praying to God for him to be released.

The night before Peter's trial before the Jewish people, he was bound with two chains and slept between two soldiers while more soldiers guarded the jail gate. Suddenly an angel of the Lord stood in the jail, and the room was filled with light. The angel tapped Peter on the side and woke him up.

"Hurry, get up!"

The chains fell off Peter's wrists.

The angel continued, "Get dressed, put on your clothes and sandals." Peter did as he was told.

"Put on your coat and follow me," said the angel.

The angel went out and Peter followed him out of the prison, but he had no idea what was really happening — he thought he was seeing a vision. Peter and the angel went past the first guard and the second guard. Then they came to the iron gate that separated the jail from the city. The gate opened for them by itself. After they went through the gate and walked for about a block, the length of a street, the angel disappeared and left him.

Peter finally realised what had happened.

"Now I know that the Lord truly sent his angel to rescue me from King Herod and from everything those Jews thought would happen to me."

Peter made his way to the home of Mary, the mother of John Mark. Many people were gathered in her house and they were praying. Peter knocked at the outer entrance, and a servant girl named Rhoda came to answer the door.

She recognised Peter's voice and was so happy that she forgot to open the door for Peter. She ran inside the house and shouted, "Peter is at the door!"

The believers said to her, "You are crazy!"

She kept insisting that it was true. So they said, "It must be Peter's angel."

Peter kept on knocking and after a while, the believers opened the door and saw him. They were astonished. Peter made a sign with his hand to tell them to be quiet. He explained to them how the angel of the Lord led him out of the jail.

"Tell James and the other brothers what happened," he said and left for another place.

The next morning, the soldiers were greatly distressed because Peter was missing. King Herod searched everywhere for him but could not find him. So he questioned the guards and ordered that they be killed.

Further reading; Acts 12:1-18, Mark 11:24, James 5:13.

☀ Highlights

PRAYER - Rhoda was a servant girl with a pure and joyful heart that was clearly seen when she saw Peter at the door. In those times, it was very challenging to live and share your faith as a Christian. Although she was a servant girl, she did not allow her life circumstances to make her timid. She saw herself exactly how God saw her. She was the first to witness the answers to the prayers offered to God for Peter's release from jail.

God truly answers prayers. It does not matter how difficult the situation may be. All you have to do is trust him and when necessary, join your faith with other believing like-minded Christians. Have confidence that God hears you whenever you ask for anything according to his will.

ENCOURAGER - Rhoda had faith — she believed it was Peter she saw at the door even though others did not. She had no doubt on what she had seen and was insistent. Because of this, the group finally believed her. They were all astonished when they set their eyes on Peter.

With God, all things are indeed possible! How wonderful would it be if you could think of ways to motivate and encourage others.

Ponder

- When I pray, do I truly believe God would hear and answer my prayers?

- In what ways can I encourage others?

Declare

- When I am troubled I pray to you Lord. When I am happy I sing songs of praise. I am confident that God answers me.

- I live by faith in God and not in what I can see.

MY NOTES

MY NOTES

TIMOTHY

1 Timothy 4:12 You are young, but don't let anyone treat you as if you are not important. Be an example to show the believers how they should live. Show them by what you say, by the way you live, by your love, by your faith, and by your pure life.

This was Paul's instruction to Timothy.

Timothy was a young disciple of Christ. He met Paul, the Apostle, during Paul's mission trip to the city of Lystra. Timothy was well known in his city and the believers had good things to say about him. His father was Greek, while his mother, Eunice and grandmother, Lois were Jewish Christians. His mother and grandmother were his first godly influences, as they helped shape his life and build his faith in Christ.

Paul the Apostle taught and mentored Timothy, and treated him like a son. He eventually became Paul's close companion and missionary colleague. As a young minister of the gospel, Paul sent Timothy to lead in the Ephesian Church. Paul was not always present with Timothy, but he could trust him to lead because he had equipped him with knowledge during the times they had spent together.

One of the challenges Timothy faced as a leader was that he was looked down on by older people because of how young he was.
The challenges Timothy encountered inspired Paul to write letters of encouragement and instructions to him. These letters are seen in the first and second books of Timothy in the bible. These letters were addressed to Timothy, the leaders of the church, and Christian believers everywhere.

The church in Ephesus had a problem — there were false teachers of the gospel of Christ who changed the truth of God's word. These false teachings began to spread fast in the church and Timothy alongside other strong believers had to guard against them. They rejected any contrary teachings to the word of God by knowing the truth of God's word for themselves and by preaching to others. Paul advised Timothy to concentrate on his personal development and to ensure that he and his hearers were saved.

Paul always prayed for Timothy. Timothy was shy and timid and needed lots of encouragement, which Paul provided. He encouraged Timothy to grow, develop and use his special spiritual gifts to serve God.

In those times, people were abused and oppressed for preaching the gospel. Sometimes, they were arrested or even killed. Timothy may have been afraid for his own life, especially because Paul, his mentor, was imprisoned for preaching the gospel and was writing to him from jail.
Now, we as children of God have the liberty to preach the gospel of Christ. In some parts of the world, however, it is still impossible or very difficult to talk about God's word. This is why we must pray for the light of God to reach every part of the world.

Further reading; I Timothy, 2 Timothy.

Highlights

MENTORSHIP - Paul and Timothy had a healthy and thriving mentor and mentee / spiritual father and son relationship. Paul saw the gift of God in Timothy and never gave up on him regardless of his weaknesses and mistakes. He prayed and thanked God daily for Timothy. Timothy needed the relationship he had with Paul to be an effective steward of his God-given gifts. Timothy was humble. He honoured Paul the Apostle and served diligently.

A mentor is a person that helps, guides, encourages and supports you so you can develop into the best version of yourself. Mentors do all these by listening, asking relevant questions, giving constructive feedback, providing relevant advice, information and guidance required in your journey.

A mentor is different from a coach, trainer, or teacher. You can have different mentors for different key areas of your life. Mentoring is important and it should be flexible. A mentor/mentee relationship should be a healthy and respectful one, so choose wisely. As you receive from your mentor, find different ways to serve and give back to your mentor. Honour and give your mentors grace when they make errors. Although they are experienced, remember, your mentor is not perfect and has flaws too.

BACKGROUND - Timothy was raised by a godly mother and grandmother and this had a significant influence on his life. He wasn't perfect and he had his weaknesses. Nonetheless, he had great values and he was well known for them in his city.

If you don't have a godly background, you are special. Jesus wants a relationship with you and he wants you to come to him just as you are. Remember to bring along others in your family and community too! When you receive Jesus into your heart, he transforms your life and gives it meaning. If you have godly parents or guardians and you are being raised as a believer in Christ, do not take your circumstance for granted. Make the most of where you are. This would make you wise and build you into who God has called you to be. Do not forget to share the gospel of Jesus with your friends.

DISCIPLE - Young Timothy was a follower of Christ. He studied holy scriptures from his childhood and continued to do so as an adult. He also learned a lot from his mentor Paul. All these gave Timothy a good foundation as a teacher of the word of God. He helped all those that were confused about the truth of God's Word. It was easy for people to look down on him or intimidate him because of his age, but he did not treat this as an excuse to stop preaching. Instead, he earned their respect.

Let Timothy be an example for you to learn from,

especially how he lived, loved people, trusted God and did the right things. Study God's word for yourself to know him better. Start from a verse daily and make it a habit. With time, you will build on this habit, and read more verses and chapters of the bible.

The bible is 'God breathed' — it was written by men but completely inspired by God, so every word in it is powerful.

There are still false teachers in the world who confuse a lot of people. When you meet them, don't get carried away arguing with them. Remember, you are to help anyone who is confused about the truth of God's word. Loving God may cost you your popularity or time, but it is well worth any sacrifice you will ever make.

AGE - Although the bible did not give Timothy's exact age, it laid a lot of emphasis on the fact that he was young.

Regardless of your age, God can use you. Give Jesus your heart and study his word. You do not need to have all the answers to follow Christ. As God directs you, be prepared to obey him. Surround yourself with godly people who would encourage you in your journey as a believer. You cannot grow in isolation as a believer. When it gets challenging, do not give up but press on. We have the Holy Spirit as our helper and comforter.

Ponder

- Who is my mentor?

- How can I start studying God's word more?

- In what ways can I share the gospel and my faith with others?

- Do I live my life daily as an example to other believers?

Declare

- Help me Lord to not be tired of doing good.

- Lord, give me the boldness to tell others about you.

- God has not given me the spirit of fear, but that of power and of love. I have a sound mind.

- Help me Lord to be an example of a believer in what I say and do.

MY NOTES

MY NOTES

MARY, THE MOTHER OF JESUS

Mary was a young teenage virgin girl who lived in Nazareth, a town in Galilee. She was engaged to marry a man called Joseph. Both of them were descendants of King David.

One day God sent an angel, Gabriel, to deliver an important message to Mary.

Luke 1

28 The angel came to her and said, "Greetings! The Lord is with you; you are very special to him."
29 But Mary was very confused about what the angel said. She wondered, "What does this mean?"
30 The angel said to her, "Don't be afraid, Mary, because God is very pleased with you.
31 Listen! You will become pregnant and have a baby boy. You will name him Jesus.

32 He will be great. People will call him the Son of the Most High God, and the Lord God will make him king like his ancestor David.

33 He will rule over the people of Jacob forever; his kingdom will never end."

34 Mary said to the angel, "How will this happen? I am still a virgin."

35 The angel said to Mary, "The Holy Spirit will come to you, and the power of the Most High God will cover you. The baby will be holy and will be called the Son of God.

36 And here's something else: Your relative Elizabeth is pregnant. She is very old, but she is going to have a son. Everyone thought she could not have a baby, but she has been pregnant now for six months.

37 God can do anything!"

38 Mary said, "I am the Lord's servant. Let this thing you have said happen to me!" Then the angel went away.

39 Mary got up and went quickly to a town in the hill country of Judea.

40 She went into Zechariah's house and greeted Elizabeth.

41 When Elizabeth heard Mary's greeting, the unborn

baby inside her jumped, and she was filled with the Holy Spirit.

42 In a loud voice she said to Mary, "God has blessed you more than any other woman. And God has blessed the baby you will have.

43 You are the mother of my Lord, and you have come to me! Why has something so good happened to me?

44 When I heard your voice, the baby inside me jumped with joy.

45 Great blessings are yours because you believed what the Lord said to you! You believed this would happen."

Mary's song

46 Then Mary said,

"I praise the Lord with all my heart.

47 I am very happy because God is my Savior.

48 I am not important,

   but he has shown his care for me, his lowly servant.

From now until the end of time,

   people will remember how much God blessed me.

49 Yes, the Powerful One has done great things for me.

   His name is very holy.

50 He always gives mercy

   to those who worship him.

51 He reached out his arm and showed his power.

   He scattered those who are proud and think great things about themselves.

52 He brought down rulers from their thrones

   and raised up the humble people.

53 He filled the hungry with good things,

   but he sent the rich away with nothing.

54 God has helped Israel—the people he chose to serve him.

   He did not forget his promise to give us his mercy.

55 He has done what he promised to our ancestors,

   to Abraham and his children forever."

56 Mary stayed with Elizabeth for about three months and then went home.

Joseph was a good and upright man. He was a carpenter in Nazareth. When Joseph found out that Mary was pregnant outside of wedlock, he did not want to disgrace her publicly, so he planned to break their engagement privately.

Matthew 1

20 While Joseph thought about this, an angel of the Lord came to him in a dream. The angel said, "Joseph, descendant of David, don't be afraid to take Mary as your wife. The baby in her is from the Holy Spirit.

21 She will give birth to a son. You will name the son Jesus. Give him that name because he will save his people from their sins."

22 All this happened to make clear the full meaning of what the Lord had said through the prophet:

23 "The virgin will be pregnant. She will have a son, and they will name him Immanuel." This name means "God is with us."

When Joseph woke up from the dream, he obeyed the angel of God and married Mary but he had no sexual relations with her before she gave birth to her baby.

Augustus Caesar, the Roman Emperor, gave an order that the whole Roman Empire be registered in a census. This made everyone go back to their own cities and hometowns to be registered.

Mary was heavily pregnant at the time, and she and her husband had to get registered. She travelled with Joseph from the city of Nazareth, in Galilee, to Bethlehem, the city of David, in Judea.

While they were in Bethlehem, Mary went into labour. All the inns were full and there was no room for her to deliver the child. The only available place for her was in a manger. Mary gave birth to her firstborn and it was a son. Joseph named him Jesus, just as he had been instructed to do by the angel.

Mary and Joseph continued to nurture Jesus. They gave birth to other sons and daughters. Jesus' brothers were James, Joseph, Simon and Judas.

Although Mary knew Jesus Christ, her firstborn son, was the Saviour of the entire world, her heart was broken and she grieved when he was crucified. She stood at the cross, with her sister, Mary the wife of Clopas, as well as Mary Magdalene.

John 19
26 Jesus saw his mother. He also saw the follower he loved very much standing there. He said to his mother, "Dear woman, here is your son."
27 Then he said to the follower, "Here is your mother." So after that, this follower took Jesus' mother to live in his home.

Further reading; Luke 1 & 2, Matthew 1: 18-25, 13:55-56, John 19.

☀ Highlights

DEVOUT - Mary was God fearing. She had strong faith in God and believed him even when she did not fully understand what was happening. As a young girl, even before she became the mother of Jesus, she lived a pure and holy life. Have you ever wondered, "Was Mary the only young girl that was a descendant of David during that season? Why was she the one that was chosen?"

Living in chastity may seem unpopular in our present culture but God has his expectations and will not lower his standards. Regardless of the many societal pressures, remember that God still honours purity and you live for your Maker. It is the pure in heart that will see God, so consecrate yourself as preparation of what would be birthed through you for the glory of God.

Psalm 119

9 How can a young person live a pure life?
   By obeying your word.
10 I try with all my heart to serve you.
   Help me obey your commands.
11 I study your teachings very carefully
   so that I will not sin against you.

HUMILITY - God chose a simple and lowly girl to be the mother of the Messiah. Before anyone can disqualify themselves as not being fit or qualified enough to be used by God, they should realise God's standards are different.

Even though she was the mother of Jesus Christ, the Saviour of the entire world she remained humble. God is opposed to proud people and he gives grace to the humble. Be humble!

FAITH & COURAGE - An angel of the Lord was sent to deliver a message to Mary. She accepted the call to give birth to the Messiah even though she was unsure about how her life would turn out. She trusted that God's plans would be nothing compared to her own plans and would ultimately be way better. She had the courage to surrender.

God wants you to trust him with all your heart, not just some part of it. Step out in faith!

OBEDIENT - Mary obeyed God's call on her life, even when she had her own plans of what she would be in future. When you trust God, you can obey what he tells you to do, because it is difficult to obey a person you do not trust. When you obey, you build your faith in God. Obeying God is better and more important to him than any sacrifice.

SURRENDER - Mary said, "Yes Lord." She agreed to let go of her ordinary plans to embrace God's extraordinary plans for her life. The question to ask is "How can this be?" and not "Will this ever be?" because with God all things are possible.

God's plan for Mary was made possible by the power of the Holy Spirit. So just like Mary, when you give God all your dreams and aspirations when you surrender your ordinary plans to God and follow him, he gives you the extraordinary life he has planned for you. God has put so much in you; he wants you to birth ideas, inventions and innovations that can transform your generation and the entire world for good.

FRUITFULNESS - Mary bore Christ the King, and the Saviour of the whole world that has redeemed mankind. God made human beings (male and female) in his image and likeness. He put us on earth to be fruitful and multiply and to reign over the living things on earth. Through you, God wants to birth ideas, witty inventions and innovations that would transform the lives of many for his glory. Will you trust Him?

Ponder

- Am I humble?

- Am I living in purity?

- In what areas of my life do I need to surrender to God completely?

- Do I have any creative ideas?

Declare

- I humble myself before God and He makes me great.

- I listen carefully, obey God's word and I do all God tells me to do.

- I am wise and I bring joy to my family and others.

- God has chosen and sent me. I bear fruit that lasts.

MY NOTES

MY NOTES

JESUS

Jesus Christ the son of God and the Saviour of the world was conceived by the power of the Holy Spirit. He was born in a manger in Bethlehem to Joseph and Mary, his earthly parents and descendants of King David.

On the night Jesus was born, some shepherds living out in the fields near Bethlehem were watching their flock of sheep, when an angel of the Lord appeared to them and the glory of God was shining all over them. The shepherds were frightened.

Luke 2

10 The angel said to them, "Don't be afraid. I have some very good news for you—news that will make everyone happy.

11 Today your Savior was born in David's town. He is the Messiah, the Lord.

12 This is how you will know him: You will find a baby wrapped in pieces of cloth and lying in a feeding box."

13 Then a huge army of angels from heaven joined the first angel, and they were all praising God, saying,

14 "Praise God in heaven, and on earth let there be peace to the people who please him."

15 The angels left the shepherds and went back to heaven. The shepherds said to each other, "Let's go to Bethlehem and see this great event the Lord has told us about."

The shepherds hurried and found Mary, Joseph and the baby lying in a manger. They told everyone what had happened and what the angel of the Lord said. Everyone that heard them was surprised. Mary, his mother, kept these things in her heart and thought about them often. The shepherds returned to their flock in the fields, praising and thanking God for all they had heard and seen.

After eight days, the baby was circumcised according to the laws of Moses and was named "Jesus".

Another law of Moses that the Jews obeyed was the ceremony of purification and when the time came for it, Jesus was taken to the temple in Jerusalem to be presented and dedicated to the Lord.

The Holy Spirit came upon him and told him, he would not die before he had seen the Messiah, Jesus Christ. On the day of the purification, the Holy Spirit led Simeon to the temple and he was there when Joseph and Mary brought baby Jesus for his dedication.

Luke 2

28 Simeon took the baby in his arms and thanked God:
29 "Now, Lord, you can let me, your servant, die in peace as you said.
30 I have seen with my own eyes how you will save your people.
31 Now all people can see your plan.
32 He is a light to show your way to the other nations.
    And he will bring honor to your people Israel."
33 Jesus' father and mother were amazed at what Simeon said about him.
34 Then Simeon blessed them and said to Mary, "Many Jews will fall and many will rise because of this boy. He will be a sign from God that some will not accept. 35 So the secret thoughts of many will be made known. And the things that happen will be painful for you—like a sword cutting through your heart."

In the temple, on that day, was also a Prophetess called Anna from the tribe of Asher. Her husband died after sonly seven years of their marriage. She remained a widow, living in the temple, and worshipping God with fasting and prayer day and night. She was eighty-four years old when she saw Jesus. Anna gave thanks to God for Jesus and she spoke about him to everyone in the temple hoping for the freedom of Jerusalem.

Jesus was also visited by some wise men from the east. People are unsure of how they heard the news about the birth of Jesus, but they followed a bright star and travelled from very far. They stopped by the palace in Jerusalem because they thought the Messiah was born in royalty. They asked King Herod who was ruling at the time where they could find the Messiah, but Herod was not aware. They continued to follow the star till they found Jesus with his mother, Mary. When they found Jesus, they were overjoyed. They fell down and worshipped him. The wise men presented Jesus with gifts of gold, myrrh and frankincense. When it was time to leave, they were warned in a dream not to return to King Herod, so they went back to their country using another route.

Not long after, Jesus and his parents returned to their hometown, Nazareth in Galilee.

Every year, Mary and Joseph went up to Jerusalem for a festival called 'Feast of Passover'. When Jesus was twelve years old, as usual, he attended the festival with his parents. When the festival was over, his parents travelled back to their hometown Nazareth. Unknown to them, Jesus stayed back in Jerusalem. It was not until after a day's journey they realised that Jesus was not in their company, and they began to look for him everywhere. They looked for him amongst their relatives and friends but they did not find him. They decided to go back to Jerusalem to look for him. After three days, they found him in the temple in Jerusalem, seated amongst teachers, listening and asking them questions.

Jesus was so wise that everyone that heard him was astonished by his intelligence, understanding and answers. When his parents found him, they were amazed. They told him how worried and anxious they were while looking for him. Jesus told them that he had to be in his father's house, but his parents did not understand his response.

Jesus followed his parents back to Nazareth and was obedient to them. Jesus continued to grow in wisdom and stature. God was pleased with him and people were pleased with him too.

So why did Jesus come to earth?

To redeem us, because He loves us.
He came to destroy the devil's work!

1 John 3:8 The devil has been sinning since the beginning. Anyone who continues to sin belongs to the devil. The Son of God came for this: to destroy the devil's work.

Jesus's cousin, John the Baptist, lived in the wilderness and he told many people to repent and ask God for forgiveness of their sins. Many people came to him. He baptised them in the river Jordan. The people thought in their hearts that John was Elijah the prophet or Christ the Messiah but he wasn't. Instead he was the forerunner of Jesus Christ.

John 1: 23 John told them the words of the prophet Isaiah: "I am the voice of someone shouting in the desert: 'Make a straight road ready for the Lord."

Luke 3:21 When all the people were being baptized, Jesus came and was baptized too. And while he was praying, the sky opened, 22 and the Holy Spirit came down on him. The Spirit looked like a real dove. Then a voice came from heaven and said, "You are my Son, the one I love. I am very pleased with you."

Jesus started his ministry on earth when he was about thirty years old. He went to the Jordan River to be baptised by John, the baptist.

After Jesus returned from his baptism in the Jordan river, he was filled with the Holy Spirit. The Spirit of God led him to the desert where the devil tempted Jesus for forty days. All through this period, Jesus fasted and did not eat any food. At the end of forty days, he overcame all the temptations by Satan. He was also very hungry.

Jesus returned to Galilee with the power of the Holy Spirit. He started teaching in the synagogue. He taught by the seaside and on land. He delivered many by casting out demons from people who were possessed. Everywhere Jesus went, he did good works. He was moved with compassion for people and healed the sick and raised the dead.

Jesus devoutly chose his disciples, who became apostles. There were twelve of them. Their names are Bartholomew, also known as Nathanael, James, the son of Alphaeus, Andrew, Judas Iscariot, Peter also known as Simon, John, Thomas, James, Philip, Matthew, Jude Thaddeus, and Simon, the Zealot.

Matthias later replaced Judas Iscariot after he betrayed Jesus. Jesus called these men while they were busy with their work and businesses to follow him, and they did. They went about with Jesus healing the sick, doing miracles and teaching the people about the kingdom of God. Jesus did a lot of teachings with parables — earthly stories with heavenly meaning — because people could relate more with them and remember the stories and their lessons easily.

Jesus' first miracle;

John 2
1 Two days later there was a wedding in the town of Cana in Galilee, and Jesus' mother was there.
2 Jesus and his followers were also invited.
3 At the wedding there was not enough wine, so Jesus' mother said to him, "They have no more wine."
4 Jesus answered, "Dear woman, why are you telling me this? It is not yet time for me to begin my work."
5 His mother said to the servants, "Do what he tells you."
6 There were six large stone waterpots there that were used by the Jews in their washing ceremonies. Each one held about 20 or 30 gallons.
7 Jesus said to the servants, "Fill the waterpots with water." So they filled them to the top.
8 Then he said to them, "Now dip out some water and take it to the man in charge of the feast."
So they did what he said.
9 Then the man in charge tasted it, but the water had

become wine. He did not know where the wine had come from, but the servants who brought the water knew. He called the bridegroom 10 and said to him, "People always serve the best wine first. Later, when the guests are drunk, they serve the cheaper wine. But you have saved the best wine until now."

11 This was the first of all the miraculous signs Jesus did. He did it in the town of Cana in Galilee. By this he showed his divine greatness, and his followers believed in him.

12 Then Jesus went to the town of Capernaum. His mother and brothers and his followers went with him. They all stayed there a few days.

Jesus was a good shepherd to his people. Everywhere he went, he did good. He had compassion for the sick and healed them. He raised the dead and performed many more miracles. This has always been God's plan for mankind and Jesus brought God's will on earth. There were times when Jesus was misunderstood. Some thought he was the Messiah while some thought he was a prophet of old.

Regardless of all the good works of Christ, not everyone loved him. Some people hated him and tried to kill him, but they could not because it was not his time yet.

From time to time, he told his disciples how much he would suffer. He told them that he must be killed and on the third day, he would be raised from death but they did not really understand the things he said.

One time, Jesus took his disciples — Peter, James, and John the brother of James — up on a high mountain. They were all alone up there. While Jesus' disciples watched him, his face changed and became bright like the sun. His clothes became white as light. Two men appeared beside him and began talking to him. Those two men were Moses and Elijah.

Matthew 17

4 Peter said to Jesus, "Lord, it is good that we are here. If you want, I will put three tents here—one for you, one for Moses, and one for Elijah."

5 While Peter was talking, a bright cloud came over them. A voice came from the cloud and said, "This is my Son, the one I love. I am very pleased with him. Obey him!"

6 The followers with Jesus heard this voice. They were very afraid, so they fell to the ground.

7 But Jesus came to them and touched them. He said, "Stand up. Don't be afraid."

8 The followers looked up, and they saw that Jesus was now alone.

9 As Jesus and the followers were coming down the mountain, he gave them this command: "Don't tell anyone about what you saw on the mountain. Wait until the Son of Man has been raised from death. Then you can tell people about what you saw."

Jesus had a triumphant entry into Jerusalem as a king;

Mathew 21
6 The followers went and did what Jesus told them to do.
7 They brought the mother donkey and the young donkey to him. They covered the donkeys with their coats, and Jesus sat on them.
8 On the way to Jerusalem, many people spread their coats on the road for Jesus. Others cut branches from the trees and spread them on the road.
9 Some of the people were walking ahead of Jesus. Others were walking behind him. They all shouted, "Praise to the Son of David!
    'Welcome! God bless the one who comes in the name of the Lord!'
Praise to God in heaven!'"
10 Then Jesus went into Jerusalem. All the people in the

city were confused. They asked, "Who is this man?"

11 The crowds following Jesus answered, "This is Jesus. He is the prophet from the town of Nazareth in Galilee."

Jesus' ministry on earth lasted for about three years. Towards the end, he comforted his disciples.

John 14
1 Jesus said, "Don't be troubled. Trust in God, and trust in me.
2 There are many rooms in my Father's house. I would not tell you this if it were not true. I am going there to prepare a place for you.
3 After I go and prepare a place for you, I will come back. Then I will take you with me, so that you can be where I am.

Matthew 26
17 On the first day of the Festival of Unleavened Bread, the followers came to Jesus. They said, "We will prepare everything for you to eat the Passover meal. Where do you want us to have the meal?"
18 Jesus answered, "Go into the city. Go to a man I

know. Tell him that the Teacher says, 'The chosen time is near. I will have the Passover meal with my followers at your house.'"

19 They obeyed and did what Jesus told them to do. They prepared the Passover meal.

20 In the evening Jesus was at the table with the twelve followers.

21 They were all eating. Then Jesus said, "Believe me when I say that one of you twelve here will hand me over to my enemies."

22 The followers were very sad to hear this. Each one said, "Lord, surely I am not the one!"

23 Jesus answered, "One who has dipped his bread in the same bowl with me will be the one to hand me over.

24 The Son of Man will suffer what the Scriptures say will happen to him. But it will be very bad for the one who hands over the Son of Man to be killed. It would be better for him if he had never been born."

25 Then Judas, the very one who would hand him over, said to Jesus, "Teacher, surely I am not the one you are talking about, am I?"

Jesus answered, "Yes, it is you."

26 While they were eating, Jesus took some bread and thanked God for it. He broke off some pieces, gave them

to his followers and said, "Take this bread and eat it. It is my body."

27 Then he took a cup of wine, thanked God for it, and gave it to them. He said, "Each one of you drink some of it.

28 This wine is my blood, which will be poured out to forgive the sins of many and begin the new agreement from God to his people. 29 I want you to know, I will not drink this wine again until that day when we are together in my Father's kingdom and the wine is new. Then I will drink it again with you."

30 They all sang a song and then went out to the Mount of Olives.

Jesus prayed for his disciples. While in the Garden of Gethsemane, one of his disciples, Judas Iscariot, came with a crowd of armed men and he betrayed Jesus with a kiss.

Matthew 26

48 Judas planned to do something to show them which one was Jesus. He said, "The one I kiss will be Jesus. Arrest him."

49 So he went to Jesus and said, "Hello, Teacher!" Then Judas kissed him.

50 Jesus answered, "Friend, do the thing you came to do." Then the men came and grabbed Jesus and arrested him.

From the time Jesus was arrested till the time he was crucified on the cross and buried in a tomb, he was ridiculed and suffered a lot of pain. On the third day, after his death and burial, he rose from the dead. That day, Mary Magdalene and another woman, also named Mary, went to the tomb of Jesus.

Matthew 28

5 The angel said to the women, "Don't be afraid. I know you are looking for Jesus, the one who was killed on the cross.

6 But he is not here. He has risen from death, as he said he would. Come and see the place where his body was.

7 And go quickly and tell his followers, 'Jesus has risen from death. He is going into Galilee and will be there before you. You will see him there.'" Then the angel said, "Now I have told you."

Jesus appeared to His disciples after resurrection and comforted them.

John 20

19 The day was Sunday, and that same evening the

followers were together. They had the doors locked because they were afraid of the Jewish leaders. Suddenly, Jesus was standing there among them. He said, "Peace be with you!"

20 As soon as he said this, he showed them his hands and his side. When the followers saw the Lord, they were very happy.

21 Then Jesus said again, "Peace be with you. It was the Father who sent me, and I am now sending you in the same way."

22 Then he breathed on them and said, "Receive the Holy Spirit. 23 If you forgive the sins of anyone, their sins are forgiven. If there is anyone whose sins you don't forgive, their sins are not forgiven."

Jesus spent forty days on earth after his resurrection from the dead.

Acts 1

6 The apostles were all together. They asked Jesus, "Lord, is this the time for you to give the people of Israel their kingdom again?"

7 Jesus said to them, "The Father is the only one who has the authority to decide dates and times. They are not for you to know.

8 But the Holy Spirit will come on you and give you power. You will be my witnesses. You will tell people everywhere about me—in Jerusalem, in the rest of Judea, in Samaria, and in every part of the world."

9 After Jesus said this, he was lifted up into the sky. While they were watching, he went into a cloud, and they could not see him. 10 They were staring into the sky where he had gone. Suddenly two men wearing white clothes were standing beside them.

11 They said, "Men from Galilee, why are you standing here looking into the sky? You saw Jesus carried away from you into heaven. He will come back in the same way you saw him go."

Do you feel a lot of pressure trying to keep up with peers or pop culture? Take it to Jesus, because He says:

Matthew 11

28 "Come to me all of you who are tired from the heavy burden you have been forced to carry. I will give you rest.

29 Accept my teaching. Learn from me. I am gentle and humble in spirit. And you will be able to get some rest.

30 Yes, the teaching that I ask you to accept is easy.

The load I give you to carry is light."

Jesus Christ is and can be all to you when you invite him.

John 5

5 "I am the vine, and you are the branches. If you stay joined to me, and I to you, you will produce plenty of fruit. But separated from me you won't be able to do anything.

John 6

35 Then Jesus said, "I am the bread that gives life. No one who comes to me will ever be hungry. No one who believes in me will ever be thirsty.

36 I told you before that you have seen me, and still you don't believe.

37 The Father gives me my people. Every one of them will come to me. I will always accept them.

38 I came down from heaven to do what God wants, not what I want.

39 I must not lose anyone God has given me. But I must raise them up on the last day. This is what the one who sent me wants me to do.

40 Everyone who sees the Son and believes in him has

eternal life. I will raise them up on the last day. This is what my Father wants."

Have you wondered why you should invite Christ Jesus into your heart? Here is the reason why:

John 14
6 Jesus answered, "I am the way, the truth, and the life. The only way to the Father is through me.

John 3
1 There was a man named Nicodemus, one of the Pharisees. He was an important Jewish leader.
2 One night he came to Jesus and said, "Teacher, we know that you are a teacher sent from God. No one can do these miraculous signs that you do unless they have God's help."
3 Jesus answered, "I assure you, everyone must be born again. Anyone who is not born again cannot be in God's kingdom."
4 Nicodemus said, "How can a man who is already old be born again? Can he go back into his mother's womb and be born a second time?"
5 Jesus answered, "Believe me when I say that everyone

must be born from water and the Spirit. Anyone who is not born from water and the Spirit cannot enter God's kingdom.

6 The only life people get from their human parents is physical. But the new life that the Spirit gives a person is spiritual.

7 Don't be surprised that I told you, 'You must be born again.'

8 The wind blows wherever it wants to. You hear it, but you don't know where it is coming from or where it is going. It is the same with everyone who is born from the Spirit."

9 Nicodemus asked, "How is all this possible?"

10 Jesus said, "You are an important teacher of Israel, and you still don't understand these things?

11 The truth is, we talk about what we know. We tell about what we have seen. But you people don't accept what we tell you.

12 I have told you about things here on earth, but you do not believe me. So I'm sure you will not believe me if I tell you about heavenly things!

13 The only one who has ever gone up to heaven is the one who came down from heaven—the Son of Man.

14 "Moses lifted up the snake in the desert. It is the same with the Son of Man. He must be lifted up too.
15 Then everyone who believes in him can have eternal life."
16 Yes, God loved the world so much that he gave his only Son, so that everyone who believes in him would not be lost but have eternal life.
17 God sent his Son into the world. He did not send him to judge the world guilty, but to save the world through him.
18 People who believe in God's Son are not judged guilty. But people who do not believe are already judged, because they have not believed in God's only Son.
19 They are judged by this fact: The light has come into the world. But they did not want light. They wanted darkness, because they were doing evil things.
20 Everyone who does evil hates the light. They will not come to the light, because the light will show all the bad things they have done.
21 But anyone who follows the true way comes to the light. Then the light will show that whatever they have done was done through God.

You do not have to struggle to live as a believer, because Jesus has promised that the Holy Spirit will help you:

John 14

23 Jesus answered, "All who love me will obey my teaching. My Father will love them. My Father and I will come to them and live with them.

24 But anyone who does not love me does not obey my teaching. This teaching that you hear is not really mine. It is from my Father who sent me.

25 "I have told you all these things while I am with you.

26 But the Helper will teach you everything and cause you to remember all that I told you. This Helper is the Holy Spirit that the Father will send in my name.

27 "I leave you peace. It is my own peace I give you. I give you peace in a different way than the world does. So don't be troubled. Don't be afraid.

28 You heard me say to you, 'I am leaving, but I will come back to you.' If you loved me, you would be happy that I am going back to the Father, because the Father is greater than I am.

29 I have told you this now, before it happens. Then when it happens, you will believe.
30 "I will not talk with you much longer. The ruler of this world is coming. He has no power over me.
31 But the world must know that I love the Father. So I do exactly what the Father told me to do.
"Come now, let's go."

Further reading; Matthew 1-28, Luke 2 - 24, John 1- 20.

☀ Highlights

LIFE, SALVATION & WORSHIP - Just as the wise men looked for Jesus, so also should we go looking for Jesus. When you find him, worship him, and remember to use your gifts too.

Jesus paid the price for the salvation of the whole world when he died on the cross. When you receive Christ into your heart, you have a new life like your Saviour. You begin a new path and journey of hope. Whoever accepts Christ and believes in him will have eternal life.

Romans 10
9 If you openly say, "Jesus is Lord" and believe in your heart that God raised him from death, you will be saved.

AUTHORITY - Jesus has all the authority in heaven and on earth and so do we. We have authority over Satan and all his works when we serve Jesus.

How?
When you submit yourself to God's authority and you resist the devil, he will flee from you.

Luke 10
18 Jesus said to them, "I saw Satan falling like lightning from the sky.

19 He is the enemy, but know that I have given you more power than he has. I have given you power to crush his snakes and scorpions under your feet. Nothing will hurt you.

FAITH - Whoever believes in the name of Jesus will have eternal life.
Without faith, you cannot please God. Ask God to increase your faith in him. When we talk to God in prayer or take the holy communion, we do it by faith. We eat the body of Christ and drink his blood in remembrance of him.

OBEDIENCE - Jesus was obedient to our heavenly father. This was evident because he only did what he saw the father do. Jesus was also obedient to his earthly parents. When they found him in the temple after three days, he obeyed them and followed them home. He was also obedient to his mother who asked him to perform his first miracle to turn water into wine.

HUMILITY - Jesus, the Son of God, came into the world through the womb of a humble woman, and was born in a manger; a humble setting. A manger is not a pleasant setting with the smell and noise of animals, yet Jesus the Messiah King was born there and not in a royal palace. Jesus was a servant leader, he served both rich and poor, old and young. And he expects us to live humble lives, serving others.

Mark 10

45 Follow my example: Even the Son of Man did not come for people to serve him. He came to serve others and to give his life to save many people."

HONOUR - Jesus honoured God as well as his parents. Christ also honoured people as he taught the multitude, fed them, cast out demons that kept people afflicted and healed many that were sick. Christ expects us to honour all people too in what we say and do to them.

John 15

22 "Also, the Father judges no one. He has given the Son power to do all the judging.

23 God did this so that all people will respect the Son the same as they respect the Father. Anyone who does not respect the Son does not respect the Father. He is the one who sent the Son.

DISCIPLESHIP - Jesus carefully called and chose his disciples, and that is the way he has called you too. He calls you to follow and abide in him. He is a good shepherd and as his sheep, to hear and obey his voice. Practice listening to God's voice. Sometimes you may not understand his instructions, but your obedience to God builds your faith and shows you more of who God is.

The gift of the Holy Spirit - The third person in the Holy Trinity is gentle; there is no junior Holy Spirit. He works in and through any willing vessel if you yield to him. Follow Christ unashamedly and don't worry whether or not it sounds cool saying 'I am a Christian' or 'I am a believer.' Don't worry if people don't treat you nicely.
Why? Because Jesus says:

"People will insult you and hurt you. They will lie and say all kinds of evil things about you because you follow me. But when they do that, know that great blessings belong to you.
Mathew 5: 11

IDENTITY - Jesus was confident in who he was.
When you don't know who you are, you settle for less than you deserve. Study a verse and stories in the bible to see who God says you are. Pray and believe it.

Ponder

- Am I too young to study my bible and preach the gospel?

- Am I too young to pray and believe for others?

- Am I too young to receive Christ into my life as Saviour?

Now I would like to invite you to a journey of intimacy with Jesus.
Invite him into your heart as your Lord and Saviour. Please with your whole heart confess below:

🗣 Declare

Lord Jesus, I repent of all my sins and I ask for Your mercy and forgiveness. Please come into my heart and be my Lord and Saviour. From today I choose to live for You all the days of my life in Jesus name,

Amen.

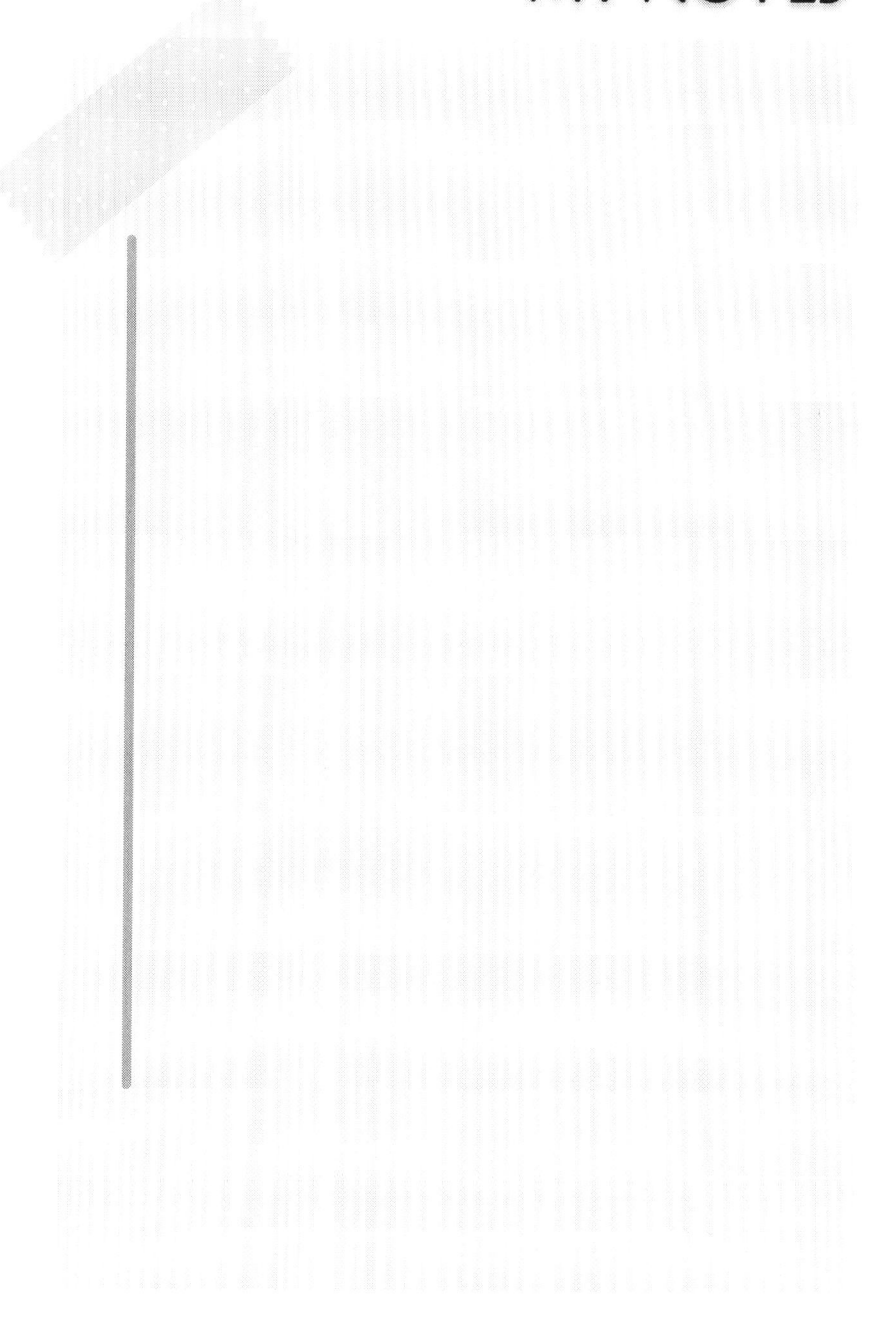

MY NOTES

MY NOTES

Are you too young then?

From the different stories you have read through, you may see yourself in one or more situations the characters also found themselves. They were imperfect but God used them, and they did great things for God. I believe that for you reading this, God would do great things in you and with you if you let him. Jesus can use you too if you decide to give him your heart and follow him.

Someone reading may say I don't have a Christian background or I don't know if this would even be a cool way of living. Understand that you have to know Jesus for yourself and say yes to a relationship with him. The Holy Spirit is our teacher, helper, comforter. Once we receive Jesus and desire the Holy Spirit, he fills us.

After reading this book, you may think;
Their lives hurt and are not as beautiful or as perfect as I want mine to be. That is fine.
Remember, there is no such thing as a perfect life without its challenges. As we get older, we will be faced with challenges and God has promised never to leave us because will see us through, but you need to know him for yourself.

Someone reading may think;
I can relate to some of the difficulties faced by these young people. Please be reassured that your story would end well and God has a perfect plan for you.

Don't be discouraged.

I encourage you to continue making faith declarations over yourself.

Job 22:28 (NKJV)
You will also declare a thing, And it will be established for you; So light will shine on your ways.

Your personality is God-given, so accept and love whom God made you to be, whether quiet or chatty. You are unique! God made only one of you; no duplicates. Even identical twins that look so similar have their own uniqueness. Do not trivialise your spiritual privilege and inheritance because they are very important in life. Don't sell your birthright so you won't regret it in the future

You are born to lead. I hope you have learned how to get it right as you read this book. Just like King Josiah, make a positive impact and leave a legacy behind.

Samuel and David had beautiful fellowship with God — they spent time with God. They knew the will of God and they brought it to pass on earth. Samuel reigned as a judge and David reigned as a king on earth. God is calling you to fellowship with him, minister on his behalf to the world, and reign with the gifts he has given you, in the purpose, he has called you to fulfil.
It's okay to be unpopular. What is most important is

that you please God.

If you must trend, ensure you represent values that honour God and you should be a positive influence on others and bring God glory.

If Jesus can use the unnamed young boy's packed lunch to serve many people, he can use and multiply whatever you give him freely. You are not lost in the crowd of life. You have something to offer Jesus that he can also multiply. What do you have that Jesus can use? It could be your voice, writing, painting or drawing.

But I am young, who will notice me?
Remember how the boy with his lunch stood out in the midst of the multitude. Jesus used the little he had and turned it into a lot.

If you feel confused about what he can use, why not pray and ask God to show you? God is our maker. He knows what we have and what he can use.

Just like Jeremiah, you are called and chosen. You are special to God. There is a purpose and reason why God chose you to be on earth and a part of your generation.

Like Joseph, make a choice to be a person of integrity, sharpen the gifts God has given you while preparing for the opportunity and when it presents itself, use it and see how successful God will make you for his glory.

Like the servant girls, don't be timid regardless of your situation. Be bold and confident, you can encourage others and be a source of great help God can use for them.

Every leader in government or any sector was once a child. Like the young kings, you have your own territory allocated to you. You are born to lead. Regardless of whether you are leading your siblings at the moment, or you lead a team at school, or a monitor in school, be humble, wise and courageous like Esther and Mordecai. You are not too young to lead your siblings, lead amongst your friends and relatives, or lead in a project whether in school, in the community or wherever you volunteer for a good cause such as fighting against cyberbullying.

Lead by example like Timothy. Ask God to show and lead you to your mentors and lead your mentors to you. Be humble enough to serve and honour all people. Those in authority over you require double honour.

You have a personal responsibility to build yourself. Have the right values to influence others positively and lead by example.

Study God's word for yourself. Start with a verse a day, a chapter a day, a Bible character, or a book in the bible. Start however you can and grow. When you are unsure about anything, ask trustworthy family, friends and your spiritual authority questions. Discuss scriptures and how practical and applicable they are to your everyday lives because God wants to be part of all you do.

Remember to meditate on God's word. Talk about the word, and keep it in your heart like David did and be careful to do all it says.

Live each day completely surrendered to God's will for you. This does not mean you won't be responsible and work hard, but that you choose to trust God and hold on to his promises for you by taking all your dreams and aspirations of life and placing it in his hands. Like Mary, you should say, "Let it be to me according to your word".

Remember, the life you have is what God has given but how you choose to live depends on you. So whether you have always known the Lord since childhood or you receive him today, what matters at this point is how you choose to live your life today and onwards. We make choices constantly, but it is most paramount to choose wisely.

I pray Christ Jesus is formed in you and that your faith in Him increases. May you continue to grow in wisdom and stature and in favour with God and man all the days of your life in Jesus' name.

Amen.

Are you still thinking to yourself, "Am I too young?"

I would love to hear from you!

If you need any support on this journey with Jesus please send an email to:
contact@hismasterpiece.co.uk
OR hismasterpiece@gmail.com

Follow us on Instagram:
@_amitooyoung_

You can also visit the website:
www.hismasterpiece.co.uk

Have you been encouraged by this book? Then I would love to implore you to recommend it to others!

I am sure that the good work God began in you will continue until he completes it on the day when Jesus Christ comes again.

Philippians 1: 6

Printed in Great Britain
by Amazon